365 Bible Stories and Prayers

Bible stories retold by Sean Connolly, Rachel Elliott, Kath Jewitt, Sue Graves, Jillian Harker, Richenda Milton-Daws, Michael Phipps and Gill Tavner

Original prayers written by Meryl Doney and Jan Payne

Illustrated by Giuliana Gregori, Natalie Hinrichsen, Anna Luraschi, Laura Rigo, Anna Shuttlewood, Christine Tappin, Barbara Vagnozzi
Cover artwork by Laura Rigo

Religious consultant: Nicki Copeland

First published by Parragon in 2013
Parragon
Chartist House
15–17 Trim Street
Bath BA1 1HA, UK
www.parragon.com

Project management by Bookcraft Ltd
Designed by Kathryn Davies
Edited by Cath Ard

ISBN 978-1-4723-2399-6

Printed in China

To Leonard
LOTS OF LOVE
From NANA & Pappy
25/12/2014

365 Bible Stories and Prayers

Parragon

Bath • New York • Singapore • Hong Kong • Cologne • Delhi
Melbourne • Amsterdam • Johannesburg • Shenzhen

Contents

BIBLE STORIES

The Old Testament

Contents

Contents

Contents

BIBLE STORIES
The New Testament

Contents

PRAYERS

Thank you God,
that you are
always with me.

Psalm 56

Bible Stories

The Old Testament

God Makes the World

Genesis 1:1–2:3

Long, long ago the world was dark and empty. There was no sea or land, no rivers or mountains, no forests or deserts. There was nothing at all… until God went to work.

"Let there be light," He said, and the world filled with light.

Next, God created the seas, and, in between them, He made dry land. Then He covered the land with trees and plants.

Overhead, God placed a warm sun to shine by day and a silvery moon to shine by night. He scattered billions of twinkling stars in the sky – and so the heavens were created.

But nothing lived in the world. So God filled the seas with shimmering fish. He added creeping crabs, sly sharks and huge, wallowing whales too.

Above the land, God made birds that soar and swoop, dip and loop. Beautiful butterflies, busy bees and bustling bats filled the air.

Then God created animals of every kind to live on the land.

He was pleased with His work.

God Makes People

Genesis 2

Last of all, God created the first man and woman to care for the amazing creatures He had made.

"I shall call you Adam and Eve," He told them.

When God had finished, He looked at his work and smiled. It had taken Him six long days to complete this wonderful new world, and so, on the seventh day, He rested.

Adam and Eve loved the home God had given them. It was the most beautiful place you could imagine, full of sweet-smelling plants and flowers. Sparkling streams bubbled up from the ground, and every tree was covered with delicious fruit.

It took a long time for Adam and Eve to give every animal a name... anteater, antelope, baboon, bat, bear, camel, cat, deer, dolphin, donkey, gecko, gorilla, hare... but they didn't mind. God had given them everything they needed.

The First Sin

Genesis 3

Adam and Eve were allowed to eat the fruit of all the trees in their home, the Garden of Eden, except for one.

"This is the Tree of Knowledge," God told them, pointing out a beautiful tree covered with ripe, rosy apples. "You must never touch its fruit!"

One day, a snake who lived in the garden saw Eve standing by the Tree of Knowledge. She was looking up at the juicy apples that hung from its branches. Slyly, the snake slithered up to her.

"Look at those delicious, ripe apples," it hissed. "Why don't you try one?"

Of course, Eve knew she was not allowed to touch the apples, and she told the snake so.

"S-s-smell how s-s-sweet they are," insisted the snake. "How can it harm to take just one? Go on! You know you want to!"

Eve shook her head firmly, but the snake would not give up.

“I know why God doesn’t want you to eat the apples!” it boasted. “If you do, they will give you the gift of knowledge. Then you will know everything He knows! You will know both good and evil.”

Eve looked up at the delicious fruit. She couldn’t help wondering what it would be like to know all that God knew… Reaching out, she quickly picked a juicy-looking apple and took a big bite. Then she passed it on to Adam and encouraged him to take a bite too.

From then on, things started to go wrong…

That night, when God spoke to Adam and Eve, He knew what they had done. He was angry, and told them to leave the garden forever. To make sure they couldn’t return, God sent an angel to guard the entrance.

God Tells Noah to Build an Ark

Genesis 6:9–22

In the world outside Eden, Adam and his children's children lived a different life from the one God had planned for them in Eden. Even so, God didn't forget them and never stopped loving them.

But more and more of the people forgot God and stopped loving Him. After many years, God became very unhappy. The world was not as He wanted it to be. His people had become more and more evil. He decided to put an end to it all. The world needed a new beginning.

God decided to send a huge flood to wash away everything that was bad. But there was a man called Noah who loved God. Noah and his family were good and kind, and God wanted to save them. So He gave Noah very careful instructions and told him to get ready for the flood.

God told Noah to build an enormous boat, called an ark. He told him to fill it with two of every kind of animal in the world.

Noah told his neighbours what God was planning, but they all laughed at him because there was not a lake or sea for miles around.

Noah ignored them, and set to work on the ark. He worked hard for months and months. He built an ark so big that it was as high as the tallest tree.

When the ark was finished, Noah gathered together all the creatures as God had told him.

The line of animals went on and on, but soon they were all safely on board. Then Noah loaded the ark with enough food to last for a long time.

As soon as Noah, his wife and the rest of his family were safely on board with the animals, God shut the door firmly behind them.

The Flood

Genesis 7–8

Then it began to rain – slowly at first, and then faster and harder. The rain beat down on Earth like on an enormous drum! Streams turned into rivers. Rivers flowed into seas. Soon, all the seas joined together as one. The water spread and rose across God's Earth, until not even the tops of the highest mountains could be seen. All the people and animals drowned in the flood.

It rained without stopping for forty days and forty nights. There was nothing to see but water.

At last the rain stopped and the waters began to go down. Noah sent a raven to see if there was any dry land. But there wasn't.

God's Promise

Genesis 8; 9:7–17

Noah waited seven more days, and then tried again. This time he sent a dove which returned carrying a bright, new olive leaf in its beak. Noah knew that the water was going down and that plants and trees were growing again.

Noah sent the dove out again seven days later. It did not return. Now Noah knew the floods had completely gone and it was safe to leave the ark.

Noah opened the doors of the enormous boat, and all the animals went out onto dry land.

God made Noah a promise. He promised that He would never again destroy the world.

"Whenever you see a rainbow in the sky," He said, "remember my promise and know that I will keep it."

Job and His Troubles

Job 1–42

Job was a rich and happy man, with a wife, ten children and lots of animals. But despite his wealth and good fortune, Job did not boast or brag. He was a good, kind man, who loved God with all his heart.

God was very pleased with Job. "There is no one who loves me more than Job does," He said.

"Of course Job loves you!" replied the Devil, who was jealous. "Look how much you have given him. If you took it all away, he would curse you!"

But God believed in Job. "Very well," He told the Devil. "You may test him. Then you will see just how much Job trusts me."

From that moment on, terrible things started to happen...

Robbers took Job's cattle and donkeys. Lightning killed all his sheep and shepherds. Then bands of thieves stole his camels. Worst of all, a tornado flattened Job's home and killed all of his children.

But Job did not blame God. "Lord, you gave me everything I had," he prayed, "and now You have seen fit to take it away."

The Devil was furious. "Job would soon change his mind if he was hurt!" he cried. So he gave Job a terrible and painful illness. But still Job trusted in God.

Finally, three friends came to visit Job. "God does not punish people for no reason," they said. "You must have done something very wicked. Ask God to forgive you."

Job was angry. He knew that he had done nothing wrong, but he started to feel confused. "I am suffering too much!" he thought. "Why doesn't God take pity on me?"

Then God spoke to Job: "Where were you when I created the Earth?" He asked. "Do you understand the wonders of creation? Do you have an arm like God, and can you thunder with a voice like Mine? Will you find fault with the Almighty?"

Job was ashamed. "I am nothing, Lord," he said. "I have spoken about things I do not understand. I am sorry! I should accept that You know best."

God told Job to forgive his friends for the way they had spoken, for they did not understand. Then He gave Job twice the wealth he had before, and even gave him more children.

Job felt humbled. At last, he understood God's greatness.

The Tower of Babel

Genesis 11:1–10

Time went by and Noah's family grew bigger and bigger. There were grandchildren, great-grandchildren, and great-great-grandchildren.

Noah's family began to fill the world, just as God had wanted them to do. They all spoke the same language, so everyone could talk to one another.

Some of the family travelled to Babylonia, where they made their home. They learned new skills, such as how to make bricks from mud baked hard in the sun. They stuck the bricks together with tar and built homes for themselves. They thought they were very clever.

One day, someone suggested that the Babylonians should build a tall tower. The Tower of Babel should be the tallest in the whole world. Then everyone would know how clever they were, and they would be famous all over the world. The people were excited, and quickly set to work.

But God was watching as the people built the tower. He watched the walls grow higher and higher. It made God very sad. He knew the people were not thinking about Him at all. They were only thinking about their own importance. Soon, the people of Babylonia would think they were just as great as God. They would get bigger and bigger ideas, and become as wicked as people were before the great flood.

God knew the people had to be able to talk to each other in order to finish this tower. If they spoke in different languages and couldn't tell each other what they were doing, the building would have to stop.

So God scattered the people in all directions. He made them speak in different languages so they could not understand one another. And the tall Tower of Babel? It remained unfinished forever!

God Calls Abraham

Genesis 12:1–9

One of Noah's descendants was a wealthy man called Abraham. He was a good citizen who believed in God.

One day, God told Abraham to leave his home in Ur, and move to another country. "Place your trust in me," God told him. "I will make you the father of a great nation."

Abraham didn't want to leave his comfortable home, but he trusted God, so he packed up his possessions and set off with his wife Sarah, his servants, his animals and his nephew Lot.

After many years of travelling, Abraham and his people finally reached a land called Canaan – but there was a problem. If they all stayed together, there would not be enough food and water for everyone.

"We must go our separate ways," Abraham told his nephew. "Choose where you want to settle."

God Promises Abraham a Son

Genesis 13; 15:1–6

Lot looked at the dry hills to the west, then he looked at the lush valley of the Jordan River to the east.

"I will live there!" he said selfishly, and off he went to the valley.

When Lot had gone, God spoke to Abraham. "Look about you," He said. "All the land you can see will be yours for always – the lush and the dry. You will have as many descendants as there are stars in the sky. You will be the father of a great nation, and you will have a son of your own."

Abraham and Sarah did not have any children and they were getting old. Too old to have children, they thought. But Abraham knew that God always keeps his promises.

The Three Visitors

Genesis 18:1–10

One hot day, a few years later, Abraham saw three strangers coming towards him as he sat at the opening to his tent.

"Come!" he welcomed them. "Take a rest and share our meal." So the strangers sat down in the shade. Abraham went to fetch water and asked Sarah to prepare some food.

"Thank you," said the men. "Now let us tell you something. In nine months' time your wife will have a baby son."

Sarah overheard this from where she sat in the tent and laughed out loud. "I'm far too old to have a child!" she thought.

Hearing her, one of the visitors asked why she laughed. "Nothing is too hard for the Lord," he said.

Then Abraham knew that these men were no ordinary guests. The words they spoke came from God.

Isaac is Born

Genesis 21:1–7

Even though Abraham and Sarah knew that God had promised them a child, they found it hard to believe that something so wonderful could happen. But sure enough, after nine months, God's promise came true and Sarah gave birth to a beautiful baby boy.

Abraham and Sarah were filled with joy. They had longed for a child for so many years!

Abraham said, "We shall call him Isaac," which means 'he laughs'. "It will remind us of the happiness we feel."

Every day, Abraham and Sarah watched Isaac grow, and he crawled around the tent, laughing and playing.

"One day, he will become a fine young man," said his mother proudly.

Abraham remembered what God had told him, many years before – that his children would form the beginnings of a great nation. With the birth of Isaac, he knew that this would come true.

Lot is Rescued from Sodom

Genesis 18:17–22

On the plains of Canaan were two cities called Sodom and Gomorrah. They were full of wicked people who did cruel, bad things, and this made God very angry. Finally, He decided to do something about it.

"I cannot let this wickedness continue," God told Abraham. "I must destroy Sodom and Gomorrah before the evil spreads."

"But what about the good people living there, Lord?" replied Abraham. "Please can you spare their lives?" He was thinking of his nephew, Lot, and his family, who lived in Sodom. They were the only good people in the whole city.

So that night God sent two angels disguised as travellers into Sodom to find Lot. "Tell him that he must leave the city with his family right away," He said.

But Lot didn't want to leave the city – and neither did his wife and daughters. "What about our nice house?" they complained, when they heard God's message. "What about all our fine things?"

At last, the angels persuaded them to leave – and just in time.

Lot's Wife Looks Back

Genesis 19:23–29

No sooner had Lot and his family left the city than the sky above Sodom turned the colour of blood, and the ground began to shake. A great shower of fire and burning gas started to rain down on the city.

"Run for the hills," the angels told the family. "Don't look back!"

Lot and his daughters ran for their lives, but Lot's wife could only think of everything she had left behind. She stopped running and looked back with longing at the city behind her – and was turned into a pillar of salt.

Isaac and Rebekah

Genesis 24

Many years passed, and Isaac grew into a man. One day, Abraham sent for his most faithful servant.

"Go to my homeland and find a wife for Isaac," said Abraham.

The servant loaded ten camels and set out on a long journey.

When he arrived at the place where Abraham's brother, Nahor, lived, the servant took his camels to rest at the town well.

"Please, God," he prayed, "help me to find the right wife for Isaac. Soon, the women will come to fetch water from the well. I shall ask one of them to give me a drink. If she brings water for the camels too, she will be the right wife for Isaac."

When the servant looked up, he saw a beautiful girl carrying a water jar. He asked her for a drink. She gave him the jar, and ran to fetch some water for his camels.

"What is your name?" he asked.

"I am Rebekah, the granddaughter of Nahor," she replied.

The servant soon met Rebekah's family and told them why he had come.

Although it meant leaving her family and moving far away, Rebekah agreed to go.

As soon as Isaac saw Rebekah he fell in love with her, and they were married.

Jacob and Esau are Born

Genesis 25:19–34

For many years after they were married, Isaac and Rebekah had no children. But Isaac remembered God's promise that Abraham's family would be the start of a great nation. Isaac prayed to God to send them a child.

Soon afterwards, Rebekah gave birth to twin boys, Esau and Jacob. But the two boys were very different from one another.

Esau was Isaac's favourite, and as the older brother he would be head of the family when his father died. He loved to go out hunting, and often brought home meat for the cooking pot.

Jacob, Rebekah's favourite, was much quieter. He preferred to stay at home.

One day, when Esau came in from hunting, Jacob was cooking a lentil stew.

"Please give me some of that stew," said Esau.

"All right," said Jacob, "but only if you agree that I will be the number one son and the head of the family when our father dies."

Esau must have been very hungry indeed because he said, "Yes."

Jacob Tricks Esau and Isaac

Genesis 27

Even though they were twins, Jacob and Esau didn't look alike at all. Jacob had smooth skin. He wasn't hairy like Esau. He didn't have Esau's red hair either.

As Isaac grew old, he went blind. He knew he would die soon. At that time, it was important for a dying father to bless his eldest son as the new head of the family. Isaac sent Esau out hunting, so that they could share a meal of Isaac's favourite meat before the blessing.

But Jacob remembered the bargain he had made with his brother. Esau had been so hungry after his day out hunting that he had swapped his place as the number one son for a bowl of lentil stew. Jacob wanted to be sure that he would be the one to receive Isaac's blessing.

What is more, Jacob's mother Rebekah was on his side. So Rebekah made a plan. If Jacob pretended to be Esau, Isaac would never know because he was blind. He would bless Jacob instead of Esau.

While Esau was out hunting, Rebekah told Jacob to kill two kids from the goat herd. She made a tasty stew with the meat and then wrapped the goatskins around Jacob's arms so he would feel hairy like Esau. She dressed him in Esau's clothes and then sent him to Isaac with the food.

At first, all went well. Isaac smelled the delicious food. When he reached out to touch his son, he felt the hairy arms and thought that it was Esau. But the voice sounded wrong.

"Is it really you, Esau?" Isaac asked his son.

"Yes, I am Esau," Jacob lied to his father.

So, Isaac prayed for God's blessing on Jacob, thinking that he was his eldest son.

When Esau returned and took food in to his father, he found out what had happened. He was so angry that Rebekah was afraid he would kill Jacob. She persuaded Isaac that it would be a good time for Jacob to go away to find himself a wife. This way, he would be out of danger.

Jacob's Ladder

Genesis 28:10–22

Jacob was sent to stay with his mother's brother Laban. His mother and father hoped he would marry someone from among their own people.

He set off on his journey feeling lonely and frightened. At sunset, he settled down to sleep on the ground, wrapping his cloak around him for warmth.

As he slept, Jacob had a dream. He saw a staircase reaching up to heaven, with angels moving up and down it. The angels were carrying God's messages.

Then Jacob saw God standing near him.

God said, "I am the God of Abraham and Isaac. I will make this land on which you lie your home. I will bless you and your children and your children's children. I will watch over you and look after you wherever you go and I will bring you back home to this place."

When Jacob woke up, he was very afraid. A long journey to a strange land lay ahead of him. But then he remembered the dream and felt a little better.

"If You protect me and bring me safely back home as You have said," he prayed, "You will always be my God."

Then, feeling stronger and more comforted, Jacob picked himself up and he continued on his journey. It was still many miles to his mother's home country.

Jacob Meets Laban

Genesis 29:1–14

Jacob finally arrived at the place where his mother's brother, Laban, lived, but he did not know how to find him. He saw three flocks of sheep grazing near a well. Then a very pretty girl came to the well to get water. Jacob moved the stone cover from the top of the well to help her.

The girl turned out to be Laban's younger daughter Rachel. Jacob could not believe his luck! He told her who he was and she took him to her father's house. The whole family was glad to see him and made him very welcome.

Jacob Marries Leah and Rachel

Genesis 29:15–30

Jacob's uncle Laban had two daughters. Leah, the elder, had lovely eyes, but her sister Rachel was graceful and beautiful. Jacob fell in love with Rachel.

Jacob offered to work for Laban for seven years if at the end of the time he could marry Rachel. Laban agreed, but he wanted his eldest daughter to be married first as this was the tradition, so he decided to trick Jacob.

The seven years passed quickly and the time of the marriage arrived. Laban led his daughter to the wedding, but little did Jacob know that Leah was to be married in her sister's place. She wore a thick veil so he could not see her face.

Jacob was very sad and angry when he realized he had married the wrong sister.

Later Laban agreed to let him marry Rachel as well, and Jacob had two wives. This was not unusual at that time if a man was able to provide for more than one wife.

Jacob Has Many Sons

Genesis 29:32–30:24

Leah knew that Jacob loved her sister Rachel more than he loved her and this made her sad. But soon Leah had a baby, a little boy called Reuben. Leah and Jacob were both very happy when the baby arrived.

Leah and Jacob went on to have lots more sons, but no babies came for Rachel. In time, Jacob had ten fine sons. After Reuben came Simeon, then Levi and Judah. The other sons were called Dan and Naphtali, Asher and Gad, Issachar and Zebulun. Jacob and Leah also had a daughter named Dinah.

Rachel was very sad that she had no babies at all. She prayed and prayed, and eventually God answered her prayers. Jacob and Rachel had a son called Joseph. One day, Joseph would be a great man.

Jacob Goes Back to Canaan

Genesis 32:1–21

Many years later, Jacob decided to return home to Canaan with his wives and family. But on the way, he became afraid. Jacob knew that he had treated Esau badly and he was scared of meeting his brother again. Would he be forgiven or would Esau still want to kill him?

So Jacob sent messengers ahead to find out.

On their return, the messengers told Jacob that Esau was on his way, with four hundred men.

Jacob felt sure that his brother was going to attack him. He chose some of his best animals as presents for Esau. He sent these ahead to Esau with his servants. He hoped this would make his brother feel more kindly towards him.

Alone in the camp, Jacob worried about seeing his brother again and prayed to God for help.

"You promised to look after me," he said. "Please save me from my brother."

Jacob Wrestles with God

Genesis 32:22–33

That night, Jacob was so worried that he sent his wives, children and servants across the river so that he could be alone with God.

While he was praying, a stranger appeared and began to wrestle with him. Jacob wrestled with the stranger all night long.

This stranger was God – He had come to reassure Jacob that he was doing the right thing. Before He left Jacob in the early morning, He blessed him and gave him a new name: Israel.

Jacob Meets Esau Again

Genesis 33

When Jacob saw Esau approaching with his men, the trouble that he expected did not happen. Instead, Esau rushed to meet his brother and threw his arms around him. All their old quarrels were forgotten.

God had answered Jacob's prayers.

"Seeing your welcoming face was like looking into the face of God," Jacob said to Esau, full of joy.

Many years later, Jacob's family came to be known as the 'Children of Israel' or 'Hebrews'. God's promise had been fulfilled.

Jacob's Favourite Son

Genesis 37:1–3

Jacob had a large family. By the time he was living in Canaan he had twelve sons!

Of Jacob's two wives, Rachel was his favourite. Joseph was Jacob and Rachel's son. Rachel had another baby, but sadly she died while she was giving birth to him. Jacob was heartbroken when Rachel died. He called the baby Benjamin.

In those days, the eldest son was treated in a special way. Because Joseph was Rachel's eldest son, Jacob loved him more than his other sons. He spoiled him and treated him differently.

Joseph and his brothers were shepherds, and they looked after their father's sheep. Because he was the favourite, Joseph would tell his father if ever any of his brothers had been up to no good.

Joseph's Special Coat

Genesis 37:3–4

Jacob wanted to show Joseph how much he loved him, and to show everyone just how special Joseph was. He had a beautiful coat made for him, with long sleeves and many wonderful colours. It was the kind of coat that would normally only be worn by an eldest son.

When Joseph's ten older brothers saw him in his special coat, they realized that their father loved Joseph more than he loved them. This made them sad and angry.

They were very jealous of Joseph and refused to speak to him.

Joseph's Dreams

Genesis 37:5–11

To make matters worse, Joseph insisted on telling everyone about his dreams, in which he was always the most important person.

"Listen to this dream I had," he said one day. "We were binding sheaves of grain out in the field when suddenly my sheaf rose and stood upright, while your sheaves gathered around mine and bowed down to it."

Joseph's brothers soon guessed what he meant! "So you think you are going to be king and rule over all of us?" they asked.

Soon Joseph had another dream. "Listen," he said to his brothers, "this time I dreamed that the sun and moon and eleven stars were bowing down to me."

Joseph's brothers were very angry, but all Joseph could think of was that perhaps God had chosen him to be someone special.

The Brothers' Revenge

Genesis 37:18–24

One day, Joseph's older brothers were away from home looking after the family's sheep. Jacob sent Joseph to find them and make sure that they were all right.

The brothers saw him in the distance walking towards them. He was wearing his special coat. "This is our chance to get rid of him once and for all," they said.

So, they hatched a plan to kill him. They could then pretend that a wild animal had eaten him out in the wilderness. They were tired of Joseph and his dreams.

When Joseph arrived, the brothers grabbed him. But the oldest one, Reuben, shook his head. "Let us lower him into that well and leave him there to die," he said, secretly planning to rescue Joseph later. The brothers ripped off Joseph's special coat, and lowered him into the deep, dark well.

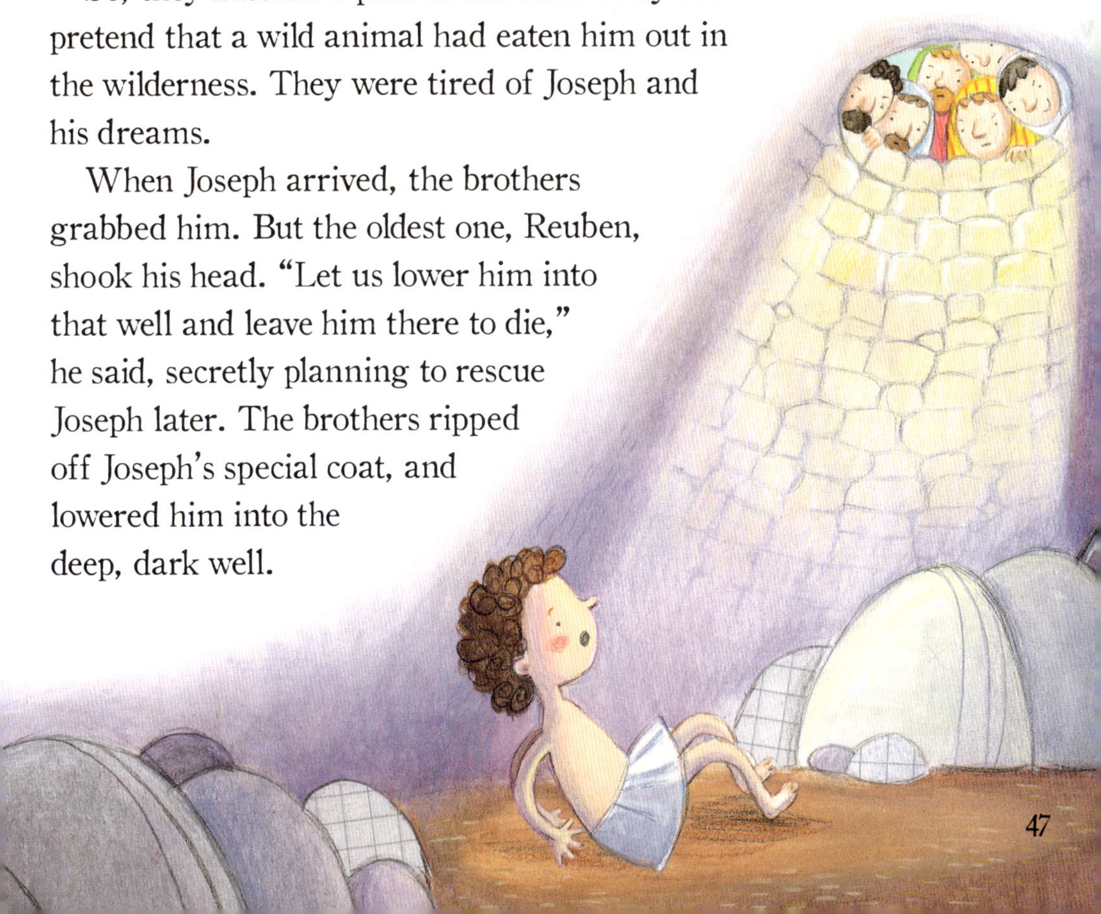

Joseph is Sold as a Slave

Genesis 37:25–35

A little later, as the brothers sat eating near the well, some spice merchants passed by on their way to Egypt. Seeing them gave Judah an idea.

"We won't gain anything if Joseph dies," he said. "Why don't we sell him as a slave?"

And so it was agreed. Joseph was dragged from the well and sold for twenty silver pieces to the next group of merchants who came along.

Then the brothers killed a goat and smeared its blood on Joseph's coat. They took the coat to Jacob.

When Jacob saw the torn and blood-stained coat, he cried out in pain. He was sure that Joseph had been killed by a wild animal.

When Joseph's brothers saw how heartbroken their father was, they were very sorry. But they didn't dare tell him what had really happened.

Joseph and Potiphar

Genesis 39

Meanwhile, in Egypt, the merchants had taken Joseph to the slave market. He was bought by a man called Potiphar, who was Captain of the Guard at the court of the Egyptian king, called the Pharaoh.

Joseph served Potiphar well. He became a trusted and loved servant. After a while, he was put in charge of his master's house and, later, all of his lands.

But before long things began to go wrong for Joseph.

Potiphar's wife was a bad woman and she decided to make trouble for Joseph. She told her husband lies, saying that Joseph had attacked her when no one was around.

Potiphar was very upset and ordered Joseph to be put in prison.

The Butler and the Baker

Genesis 40

After Joseph had been in prison for some time, two new prisoners arrived – the butler and the baker from Pharaoh's household.

One night, both of them had puzzling dreams. In the morning Joseph found them looking worried. "God can explain dreams," said Joseph. "Tell me what you saw."

The butler told Joseph that he had dreamed of a grapevine. He had squeezed the grape juice into Pharaoh's cup and given it to him to drink.

"The meaning is clear," said Joseph. "In three days, you will be free and working for Pharaoh again. Please, put in a good word for me."

Then the baker told Joseph his dream.

In this dream, the baker was carrying

three baskets full of pastries to take to Pharaoh. Birds flew down and pecked at them.

Joseph listened, and then he shook his head sadly. "This dream is bad," he said. "In three days, Pharaoh will have you killed."

Joseph was right. Three days later, the butler was back at work in Pharaoh's palace. But the baker was dead.

But as soon as the butler was released from prison, he forgot that he had promised to put in a good word for Joseph. No one came to release him – Joseph remained in prison.

Pharaoh's Dreams

Genesis 41:1–7

Two years later, Pharaoh started having strange dreams. In one dream, he was standing in a field by the Nile River when seven plump, well-fed cows came out of the water and began to feed on the grass. These were followed by seven thin, bony cows, which ate up the first cows.

Pharaoh fell asleep again and had a second dream: seven heads of grain, healthy and good, were growing on a single stalk. After them, seven other heads of grain sprouted – thin and scorched by the east wind. The thin heads of grain swallowed up the seven healthy, full heads.

Joseph is Summoned

Genesis 41:8–16

Pharaoh was very worried by his dreams so, when morning came, he sent for all the magicians and wise men in the country. Pharaoh told them about his dreams, but no one could tell him what they meant.

Then Pharaoh's butler remembered something. "A while ago," he said, "you were angry with your servants. You sent me and the chief baker to prison. One night, both of us had a dream, and each of these dreams had a special meaning."

The butler went on to tell how a young Hebrew man, Joseph, who was in prison at the same time, had listened to their dreams and told them the meaning.

"Things turned out exactly as he told us," the butler said. "I was let out of prison and given my job back, but the other man was hanged."

"If this man can explain dreams, I must see him," said Pharaoh. Immediately, Joseph was let out of prison and brought to the palace.

Joseph Explains the Dreams

Genesis 41:16–31

Then Pharaoh said to Joseph, "In my dream I was standing on the bank of the Nile, when seven cows came up from the river. They were fat and healthy, and they were eating grass at the riverbank.

Then seven more cows appeared. They were scrawny and very ugly. I had never seen such skinny cows in the whole of Egypt. These scrawny cows ate the seven fat cows all up. But even after they had eaten them, they looked just as skinny as before. Then I woke up.

In the next dream, I saw seven plump heads of corn growing on a single stalk. After them, seven dried-up heads of corn sprouted. The dried-up heads of corn swallowed up the seven plump ones. I have told all the wisest men in the land about these dreams but no one can explain them to me."

Joseph said to Pharaoh, "Both of these dreams are telling you the same thing. There will be seven years of good harvests, but seven years of bad harvests will follow. There will be famine and no food."

Joseph Becomes a Leader

Genesis 41:32–57

Joseph told Pharaoh, “You had two dreams telling you the same thing, because God has decided that it will happen. Now Pharaoh, you must look for a wise man and put him in charge of storing grain in the good years to help you through the bad.”

Pharaoh thought this was a good plan. He decided to make Joseph his chief minister. “You shall be in charge of my palace, and all my people,” he said. “Only I, Pharaoh, will be greater than you.”

Then Pharaoh gave Joseph a gold ring from his finger and dressed him in fine clothes. Joseph set to work all over the land, making sure that enough grain was stored.

Everything that Joseph had said came true. Because they had planned well, there was plenty to eat when the famine came.

Joseph's Brothers

Genesis 42:1–17

In Canaan, the famine was making life miserable for Jacob and his family. They had hardly anything to eat and were very hungry.

Jacob heard that Egypt had wheat for sale, and decided to send all his sons – except for Benjamin – to Egypt to buy some.

So the ten brothers set out on the long journey to Egypt. When they arrived they went to see Pharaoh's chief minister to ask for wheat.

The brothers did not recognize Joseph. But Joseph knew them at once! He decided to find out if they were still as cruel as they used to be.

"You are spies!" he said. The brothers tried to explain that they had come from Canaan to buy food, but Joseph ordered them to be thrown in jail.

Joseph Asks to See Benjamin

Genesis 42:16–43:15

Three days later, Joseph told them to go home and bring back their youngest brother to prove their story was true.

Joseph loved Benjamin and wanted to see him again. He kept one brother prisoner, to make sure the others would return.

Joseph ordered his servants to fill his brothers' sacks with wheat before they set off, and to secretly place the money that they had brought to pay for the wheat on top.

Back home, the brothers told Jacob everything. "We paid for the grain," said one, "but we found money in the sacks. That makes it look as if we stole it. We must go back to prove we are honest."

Jacob was terrified of losing another son, but eventually, the wheat ran out and the family went hungry. Judah begged his father to let them return, promising to look after Benjamin. At last, Jacob agreed.

Joseph fought back tears when he saw his favourite brother. He still did not want his brothers to know who he was.

The Missing Cup

Genesis 43:16–44:34

Joseph still did not want to tell his brothers who he was, but he was pleased to see them all. "Is your father well?" he asked them. As they replied, they bowed low to him – just like the sun, moon and stars had in the dream so many years before.

Joseph ordered food to be brought in. He told the servants to give more to Benjamin than to anyone else. Then the brothers' sacks were filled with food.

This time, Joseph hid his own silver cup in Benjamin's sack. The brothers set off for home, but they had not gone far when Joseph sent his guards after them to search their sacks.

When the missing cup was discovered, the horrified brothers threw themselves at Joseph's feet.

"The guilty man must stay here and be my slave. The rest of you can go!" Joseph commanded.

But Judah knew how much Jacob loved Benjamin and he was determined not to break his promise to look after him. "Please let me stay instead," he begged. "My father will die of grief if Benjamin does not return."

Reunited

Genesis 45:1–46:7

Joseph was delighted at these words. Now he knew his brothers had changed for the better. He sent his servants out of the room. "I am your brother Joseph!" he declared.

His brothers were shocked.

"It was God's plan to send me here to Egypt," Joseph explained, "so that I could look after you and many other people when the famine came. There are still five more years of bad harvests to come. Hurry home and bring the rest of the family here to live near me. We will be together again."

Joseph hugged Benjamin, then the rest of his brothers, as he cried tears of joy.

So Jacob and all of his family left Canaan and came to live in Egypt. There, he was reunited with his beloved son, Joseph.

Slavery in Egypt

Exodus 1

In Egypt, life became very difficult for the Israelite people after Joseph died. There was a new Pharaoh, who didn't know about the wonderful things Joseph had done. He thought there were too many Israelite people. He was scared they might turn against the Egyptians and try to rule the country.

Pharaoh thought that if the Israelites were forced to work hard, they would grow weak and wouldn't be able to have many children. So he turned them into slaves, working for cruel masters.

Even though the Israelites had hard lives, they were strong and healthy. Lots more Israelite babies were born. When Pharaoh saw that his plan hadn't worked, he gave a terrible order. Every Israelite baby boy would be drowned in the Nile River.

The Baby in a Basket

Exodus 2:1–10

Around this time, an Israelite woman called Jochebed had a baby boy. She knew that to save his life, she had to keep him secret. Jochebed made a basket from the reeds that grew beside the river. She covered it with tar to make it waterproof. Then she put her baby in the basket and hid it among the reeds. She told her daughter Miriam to stay nearby and watch what happened.

Later, Pharaoh's daughter came to the river to bathe. When she stepped into the water, she saw the basket and looked inside. The baby started to cry, and the kind-hearted princess felt sorry for him. She could tell that he was an Israelite.

Miriam hurried over to the princess. "Shall I find a nurse to look after the baby for you?" she asked.

Pharaoh's daughter said yes, and Miriam ran to fetch her mother. The princess asked Jochebed to care for the baby until he was old enough to live with her in Pharaoh's palace.

Moses Runs Away

Exodus 2:11–25

Pharaoh's daughter called the baby Moses. In time, Jochebed told Moses all about his people. When he grew up he looked Egyptian, but he never forgot that he was an Israelite. It made him angry to see his people treated so badly by the Egyptians. They had to work hard, digging and making bricks to build their masters fine homes.

One day, Moses saw a wicked Egyptian master beating a poor Israelite slave. He lost his temper and attacked the Egyptian. Moses was young and strong, and he hit the Egyptian so hard that the man died.

The next day, Moses saw two Israelite men fighting. He tried to stop the fight, and one of the men turned on him angrily.

"Are you going to kill me like you killed the Egyptian?" he asked.

Moses was shocked that people knew what he had done. If Pharaoh found out that he had helped an Israelite, he would be in trouble.

Moses decided to run away. He went to live in a land called Midian, where he worked as a shepherd.

Moses Helps the Priest's Daughters

Exodus 2:16–25

A priest named Jethro lived in Midian. He had once been one of Pharaoh's best advisers. But he was kind to the Israelites, so he had to leave the court and went to live in Midian.

Jethro became very important. But he soon saw that it was silly to pray to statues of false gods. He stopped being a priest.

The people of Midian turned against him. They were unkind to his daughters too, and wouldn't let them get water for their sheep. They always had to wait until everyone else had gone before they could use the well.

When Moses arrived in Midian, he saw some shepherds chasing Jethro's daughters away from the well. Moses stood up for the girls, and helped them to get water.

Jethro was surprised to see his daughters coming back from the well so soon. When they told him how Moses had helped them, Jethro invited him into his house. Moses had made a good friend.

Later, Moses married Jethro's eldest daughter, Zipporah.

The Burning Bush

Exodus 3:1–4:17

Moses spent each day in the fields, watching over Jethro's sheep and goats. One day, he took the sheep into the wilderness to graze near a mountain called Sinai. Suddenly he saw something amazing. One of the bushes was on fire, but it was not being destroyed.

Moses walked over to the bush, and then he heard a loud voice. It came from inside the bush!

"Moses! Do not come any closer," said the voice. "Take off your sandals, for the place where you are standing is holy ground."

Moses obeyed at once.

"I am the God of Abraham, Isaac and Jacob," the voice said.

Moses covered his face, because he was afraid to look at the power of God. But he listened carefully to what God said next.

"My people are suffering," said God. "I love them, and I am going to help set them free from Egypt. A wonderful new home is waiting for them in a land that flows with milk and honey. Moses, I want you to go back to Egypt. Tell Pharaoh that you have been sent to bring the people of Israel out of Egypt."

But Moses didn't want to go back.

"Don't send me," he pleaded. "No one will listen to me."

"I will be with you," said God. "When you have brought my people out of Egypt, you will give thanks here at this very place, Mount Sinai."

But Moses still looked unsure. "If I tell the people of Israel that the God of their fathers sent me to them, they might ask me for His name," he said. "What should I tell them?"

"Tell the people of Israel 'Yahweh has sent me to you.'," said God.

The name Yahweh has a very special meaning. It means that God has lived forever and God will live forever. He is God, and He loves you. Trust in Him.

"Return to Egypt," said God. "Find your brother Aaron and go with him to ask Pharaoh to set my people free."

Moses was scared of going back to Egypt, but he knew that he could not refuse his God. It was his job to lead the Israelites to the Promised Land.

Moses and Pharaoh

Exodus 5:1–6:8

Moses returned to Egypt and found his brother Aaron. They went to see Pharaoh together. They told him that God wanted His people to be released from slavery.

Pharaoh didn't believe in God. He was angry with Moses and Aaron, and he refused to free the Israelites. Instead, he gave some cruel new orders.

"Don't give the Israelite slaves any more straw to make their bricks," he commanded. "They must find their own straw, but they have to make just as many bricks as before."

Moses told God how unhappy the people were.

"Tell Pharaoh that I will make terrible disasters happen if he won't free my people," said God.

Moses and Aaron told Pharaoh what God had said. But Pharaoh didn't love God and he didn't listen. So God decided to show Pharaoh what happened when people disobeyed Him.

The Plagues

Exodus 7–10

God decided to send some terrible disasters called plagues to Egypt. First he told Aaron to touch the River Nile with his staff. When Aaron obeyed, the river water was turned to blood. All the fish died and the Egyptians couldn't drink the water.

Next, the country was overrun by giant frogs, then attacked by gigantic swarms of gnats and flies. Only Goshen, where the Israelites lived, stayed free of these creatures. Then the animals of Egypt started to die. Only the creatures in Goshen stayed healthy. But even after these plagues, Pharaoh would not let the Israelites leave Egypt.

The Egyptian people and animals started to suffer from painful lumps called boils all over their skin. Even Pharaoh was covered in boils, but his cleverest doctors could not cure him.

Pharaoh still refused to believe in God or set the Israelites free. So God sent the worst hailstorm the Egyptians had ever known. It destroyed the crops in the fields and stripped every tree bare. It was so heavy and strong that it killed the rest of the animals.

God told Moses to stretch out his hand over Egypt. He made a great wind blow across the land, and the wind brought a swarm of hungry insects called locusts. The locusts covered the land until it was black. They ate every last crop and berry in Egypt. After they had gone, there wasn't a single green plant left anywhere.

Finally, God told Moses to reach his hand up to the sky. He sent darkness over Egypt for three whole days. Only the Israelites had light in their homes.

The Passover

Exodus 11–12

The plagues had almost destroyed Egypt, but still Pharaoh would not free God's people. Moses told him that God would do one more terrible thing to the Egyptians, and then Pharaoh would free the Israelites. But Pharaoh was proud and foolish, and didn't listen.

That night, God told the Israelite families to kill a lamb or a goat and smear its blood on their front doors. Then they should roast the meat and eat it with bread made without yeast.

At midnight, God sent the angel of death to Egypt. The eldest son of every Egyptian family died. Pharaoh's son died too. But the angel of death 'passed over' any house marked with blood, because it was a sign that Israelites lived there. No Israelites died that night.

Every year afterwards, the Israelites ate a special 'Passover' meal, to remember how God saved them.

The Israelites Leave at Last

Exodus 14:5–15:21

After the death of his son, Pharaoh could not bear any more disasters. He sent for Moses and Aaron, and they came to see him at the palace.

"Leave with your people at once," said Pharaoh.

The Egyptians had suffered terrible plagues, and they were glad to see the Israelites leaving their country. But after Moses and his people had gone, Pharaoh changed his mind. Without the slaves, he had no one to do all the work. He sent his soldiers after them, hoping to stop them before they could escape.

The soldiers caught up with the Israelites at the Red Sea. At first it seemed as if the Israelites were trapped, but then Moses stretched out his arms to ask for God's help.

God sent a great wind to part the waters of the Red Sea. A dry, safe pathway opened up in front of the Israelites. They started to escape, and the soldiers followed them. But when the soldiers drove their chariots onto the pathway, the water rushed down on them and drowned every single one.

The Israelites were free at last! They danced and sang to praise God for keeping His promise and saving them from the Egyptians.

Food in the Desert

Exodus 16

The Israelites' celebrations did not last long. Soon they began grumbling about the lack of food.

"We would rather have died in Egypt, than starve to death in the desert," they moaned. But God heard them, and promised they would get the food they needed.

"You will have meat every night and bread every day, except on the Sabbath – my day of rest," He said.

That night, a huge flock of birds, called quail, flew down to where the Israelites were camped. It was easy to catch them. There was plenty of meat for everyone.

Next morning, the Israelites saw something white, flaky and as delicate as frost left behind on the ground as the dew dried.

"This is special food that God has sent for you," said Moses. "Gather as much as you need."

The food tasted sweet and appeared each morning.

The Israelites called it 'manna'.

Water in the Desert

Exodus 17:1–7

But Moses' problems did not end there. The hot sun beat down on the desert, and the people got thirstier and thirstier. There was very little water, and the Israelites started grumbling to Moses all over again. Some people got so angry they picked up large stones ready to throw at him.

Moses was afraid. He turned to God for help.

"Walk ahead with the leaders of the people," said God, "and when you reach a rock at Mount Sinai, you must hit it with your staff."

Moses did as God had told him. When he hit the rock, lots of water came gushing and gurgling out of it. The water was cool and refreshing, and everyone had plenty to drink.

So God provided food and water in the desert for his people as they journeyed back to the land of Canaan.

Moses and the Israelites

Exodus 17:8–16

Even though God had provided food and water in the desert, the Israelites continued to grumble and quarrel. But they soon discovered that there were even worse things than hunger and thirst. There were human enemies who could stop their progress to the Promised Land.

On their journey through the wilderness they came upon the Amalekite people. The Amalekites attacked the Israelites. Moses ordered a man called Joshua, whom he trusted, to gather their strongest men to fight against the Amalekites.

Joshua did as he was told and chose the strongest men to go into battle. Meanwhile, Moses took the special staff, which God had blessed, and went to seek His help.

Moses went with Aaron and Hur, his two leaders. They climbed to the top of a nearby hill where they had a good view of the battle taking place down below.

Moses held the staff of God in the air and the Israelites started to win the battle.

When his arms grew tired Moses lowered the staff and immediately the Israelites started to lose the battle.

When they saw this, Aaron and Hur found a large stone and gave it to Moses to sit on. When Moses was sitting on the stone, he was able to lift the staff once more.

Later, Moses grew tired again and his arms began to droop. Aaron and Hur quickly held his hands up – one on one side, one on the other – so that the staff was held up until sunset.

Thanks to God's help, the Israelites won the battle against the Amalekite army.

The Ten Commandments

Exodus 20

Moses and the Israelites set up camp at the foot of Mount Sinai.

God told them He had brought them there to be His chosen people.

"Will you obey Me?" He asked them.

The Israelites said they would obey Him.

Then God said He would give them ten special laws. God's laws – His 'commandments'. These laws would show the people how to serve Him properly. They would also help them to lead good lives and behave better towards one another.

Two days later, great clouds gathered, thunder rumbled and lightning flashed at the top of the mountain. Together, Moses and Aaron climbed up the mountain. When they reached the top, God gave them His ten laws.

These are the ten laws God gave His people:

Honour and serve me alone, for I am the only God.
Do not make or worship any other gods.
Treat My name with respect.
Keep every Sabbath as a day of rest.
Respect your father and mother.
Do not kill another human being.
Husbands and wives must keep their love only for each other.
Do not steal.
Do not tell lies.
Do not be greedy about things that other people have.

When God had finished speaking, He told Moses that He would give him two stone tablets, with the words of the laws carved into them. They were all the people needed to live wisely on Earth.

God's Agreement

Exodus 24–26

Because Moses was His special messenger, God explained to him how the laws worked. Moses explained the laws to the people. He told them that God loved them and that He would look after them as long as they honoured Him and obeyed His laws.

When Moses explained all this to the people they were happy and promised to obey God's laws.

After this, God asked Moses to come back up the mountain to talk with Him again. Some of the leaders went part of the way with him. They all prayed together and then Moses went on alone.

He was up at the top of the mountain talking with God for a very long time.

At the foot of the mountain, the people grew bored with waiting for Moses to return.

They went to find Aaron, Moses' brother.

"Where is Moses?" they asked him. "He has been gone so long."

The Golden Calf

Exodus 32:1–26; 34:1–4; 35

The people said to Aaron, “Moses has forgotten us, and so has his God. Make a new god to lead us.”

Aaron collected all the gold from the people, their jewellery and ornaments. He melted it down and made it into a statue of a golden bull calf.

The people worshipped this bull calf. They danced around it and sang praises. Then they had a big feast and drank.

Up on the mountain, God spoke to Moses.

“You must go back to the people,” He said. “They have broken their promises to me and have made a new god to worship.”

When they saw how quickly the people had forgotten their promises, God and Moses were really angry.

Moses threw the stone slabs, on which God had carved His laws, to the ground. They smashed into little pieces. Then Moses pulled the golden bull calf from its pedestal and ground it to powder. He mixed the gold dust with water and made the Israelites drink it.

Moses asked Aaron why he had allowed the people to make the golden statue and worship it. Aaron didn't know what to say.

Although Moses was angry, he still loved his people. He returned to the mountain to talk with God. Moses prayed to God to forgive them and He listened. God made new stone slabs – also called tablets – with the laws carved upon them. Once more, the people promised to obey God.

The Ark and the Tent

Numbers 7:1–12

To show that he would always be near them, God asked for a special tent to be made, in which the 'Ark', a wooden box covered with gold, was to be kept. This box would contain the stone tablets.

Everyone was happy to give the materials that were needed to make the tent, or 'tabernacle'. They gave all the beautiful and precious things they had. The very best craftsmen worked on God's special tent. It was beautiful, and was lined with richly coloured cloth.

Around the tent was a courtyard, where people could offer gifts such as a lamb, a kid goat or a young bull. These gifts were a way of saying sorry to God for anything they had done wrong.

God wanted to remind His people that He loved them. He knew that they were not perfect. By offering gifts to God, they could always come to say they were sorry and to give thanks.

Moses Sees God's Glory

Exodus 33:18–23

Moses went back up the mountain and asked God if He would show him His face.

God said to Moses, "No one can see My face and live. But this is what I will do for you. Go and hide behind the gap in that rock and I will walk by in all my glory. I will protect you from the sight by putting My hand across the gap in the rock. But when I have walked past, I will take My hand away from the gap in the rock, so you will be able to see My back. In this way, you will see God's glory, but not directly. It will not be too bright for you to bear, and you will live."

Moses did as God told him, and hid behind the gap in the rock until God had passed by. When God took away His protecting hand, Moses saw God's glory, but not His face. Afterwards, when Moses came back down from the mountain after seeing God, his face was shining.

The Bronze Snake

Numbers 21:4–9

Moses and the Israelites continued on their way through the wilderness. They seemed to have been wandering around for such a long time that the Israelites became very fed up. They remembered Egypt – but they only remembered the good things there: the warmth and the food, not the hard work and slavery. They complained against Moses and against God.

After a time, they came to a place where there were lots of poisonous snakes. Many people were bitten and died.

The people said to Moses, "We are sorry we have complained against God. We know we have done wrong, but please ask God to help us now."

God told Moses to make a snake out of bronze and put it on a pole.

God said, "Whenever anyone who is bitten by a poisonous snake looks at this bronze snake, he or she will live."

Moses did as God told him, and no more people died from snake bites.

Balaam's Donkey

Numbers 22

While the Israelites were camped on the plains of Moab, near the Jordan River, Balak the King of Moab started to worry. He had heard about the battles the Israelites had won.

"Fetch the wise man Balaam," he ordered his servants. "Tell him to put a terrible curse on the Israelites. That will stop them!"

When the servants arrived, Balaam listened to the King's request. "Let me think about it," he told them.

That night God spoke to Balaam. "The Israelites have my blessing," He said. "You will not be able to put a curse on them. You can go and see Balak, but only do what I tell you to do."

The next morning Balaam saddled up his donkey and off he set.

Clip! Clop! The donkey trotted happily down the road. Then, all at once, it stopped.

"Hurry up, you stupid beast!" cried Balaam, hitting the poor animal. "I have a job to do." But the donkey would not move.

Balaam was furious. He raised his stick to give the animal a beating when, through the power of God, the donkey spoke.

"Why are you hitting me?" it brayed. "Have I ever disobeyed you before?"

Suddenly, Balaam was able to see what the donkey had been able to see all along. There in the middle of the road was an angel.

"Tell Balak you are not able to curse the Israelites because God has blessed them," ordered the angel.

And those were the only words that Balaam was able to speak when he arrived. God's blessing had protected the Israelites.

God Summons Joshua

Deuteronomy 34; Joshua 1

For forty years the people of Israel lived in the desert. Moses grew old and died. He was 120 years old when he died, but he was still strong. The Israelites were very sad to have lost their leader, but God chose Joshua to be the new leader, so the Israelites listened to Joshua.

Joshua was worried about being the Israelites' leader but God told him that He would be with him. God said to Joshua: "You and your people must get ready to cross the Jordan River into the land I promised you. Do not be afraid because I will be with you wherever you go."

So Joshua ordered his officers to go through the camp and tell all the people to pack their food and belongings.

"Three days from now we will cross the Jordan River and enter the land that God has given to us," he told them.

Spies in Jericho

Joshua 2

Joshua sent two spies to the city of Jericho from their camp on the far side of the Jordan River. The city had walls all around it.

A woman called Rahab lived in a house on the city wall. She sheltered the men for the night. But the King of Jericho heard about the spies and sent his soldiers to capture them.

Rahab knew that God wanted the Israelites to have Canaan. She hid the spies on her roof. When the soldiers questioned her, she said that they had left.

"We are all afraid," Rahab told the spies. "Promise me you will keep my family safe when you take this city."

"We promise to look after you, if you promise to tell no one what we have been doing here," said the men. "Call your family together and tie a red cord to the window, so we know not to attack you. That will keep you safe."

Rahab promised to keep the men's spying a secret. Then they went back to tell Joshua what they had found out.

Crossing the Jordan

Joshua 3; 4:1–10

Soon afterwards, the Israelites got ready to cross the Jordan River to capture Jericho. But the water level in the river was high, making it too dangerous to cross. However, the priests went ahead, carrying the Ark with God's laws in it.

As soon as they stepped into the river, the banks collapsed upstream, damming the water. Now the Israelites could cross the riverbed easily.

Next the Israelites took twelve stones from the middle of the riverbed. They piled them up on the bank, as a sign of God's help in bringing them into Canaan. Then the river flooded through again.

The Israelites set up camp outside the walls of Jericho and celebrated Passover.

Joshua Takes Jericho

Joshua 6

The walls of Jericho were high and thick. Strong gates meant that no one could get in or out. Soldiers kept watch from the tall towers. How could the Israelites possibly capture such a well-defended city?

But God told Joshua exactly what to do.

"Each day, for six days, you must march around the city walls. Take my box of laws and have seven priests carrying trumpets going before the people. Tell them to blow their trumpets as you march. Everyone else must be quiet.

On the seventh day, march around the city seven times. Then the priests must play one long note on their trumpets, and all the people are to shout loudly, 'The walls of Jericho will fall and the city will be yours!'"

So Joshua called the people together and told them what God had said. "Remember, do not give a war cry, do not raise your voices, do not say a word until the day I tell you to shout. Then shout!" he said.

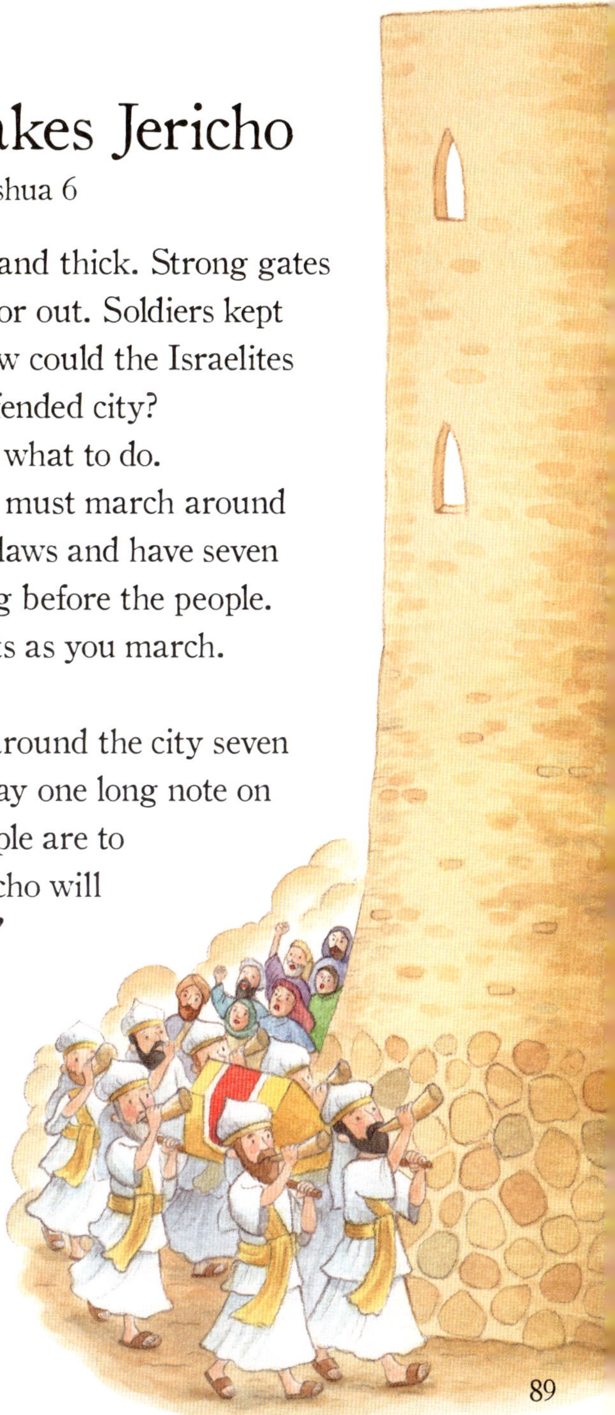

The Israelites did what God had told them to do. Each day, for six days, they marched around the walls of Jericho just as God had told them. Each night, they returned to their camp.

On the seventh day at daybreak, the Israelites came to Jericho again. They marched around the city walls once. They marched around the city twice. They continued marching as they had been told.

As they finished for the seventh time the priests sounded their trumpets with a mighty blast. Joshua gave the order for everyone to shout. The Israelites shouted as loudly as they could.

The walls of Jericho came crashing down, and the Israelites captured the city. Only Rahab and her family were saved.

The city was burnt to the ground. This was the first of Joshua's victories in Canaan.

The Day the Sun Stood Still

Joshua 10:1–14

Joshua and the Israelites went on to win many more victories in Canaan, and the Canaanite kings were all afraid. Five of them, Amorite kings from the hill country, joined forces to fight the Israelite army.

There were a great many more Canaanites than Israelites. But God said to Joshua: "Don't be afraid of them. I will look after you. None of them will be able to defeat you."

God confused the Canaanite armies and many of their soldiers ran away. As they ran, God sent a hailstorm down on them, and more of them died from the hail than were killed by the Israelite army.

Joshua commanded the sun to stand still until the battle was finished. God listened to Joshua and made the sun stand still for a whole day so that the Israelites could defeat the Canaanite armies.

Othniel and Ehud

Judges 2:16–3:20

After Joshua's death, the people of Israel forgot what God had done for them, and began to worship statues of false gods as the other tribes did. It wasn't long before things began to go wrong.

The Canaanites rose up against the Israelites, and made them pay heavy taxes. They were hard times for the people of Israel, but in their trouble they remembered God, and cried out to Him for help. And because God loved His people, He answered their prayers. He sent leaders to help and guide them, and to set Israel free. These special leaders were called judges.

The first judge was Othniel, a good man and a great warrior. Thanks to him, the people were able to live in peace for forty years. The next judge God sent to save Israel was Ehud. This time, the Moabites were forcing the Israelites to pay them a lot of money. So Ehud went to the palace and asked to see the King. When they were alone, he took out a long knife which he had hidden under his clothes, and stabbed the king. Then he brought back an army and defeated the Moabites.

Deborah

Judges 4–5

After Ehud died, the people of Israel forgot about God once again. Soon the Canaanites started to attack them and make their lives very difficult. At this time, there was a wise judge called Deborah – a woman who listened to God's word. She told a general called Barak that he should take an army of men from all the tribes of Israel up to Mount Tabor.

"From there you will be able to defeat the enemy down below," she said. Barak was terrified of the powerful Canaanite army, but he agreed, on condition that Deborah went with him.

"You must persuade the men of the other tribes to join me," he said. And Deborah did. Against all odds, the Israelites won a great victory.

An Angel Visits Gideon

Judges 6:1–24

Once again, the people of Israel were under attack. This time, their enemy was a tribe of bandits called the Midianites. As soon as harvest time came, the Midianites would swoop down and carry off animals and crops, killing anyone who got in their way. "How will we survive the winter?" cried the survivors, when the raiders had gone. "There's nothing left!"

In their misery, the Israelites cried out to God for help. And God heard their prayers. He sent an angel to visit a man named Gideon. Gideon was an ordinary chap – so he was very surprised when the angel told him that he had been chosen by God to rescue Israel.

Gideon Lays a Fleece

Judges 6:33–40

Gideon thought it was so unlikely that God had chosen him for such an important task that he decided to ask for proof.

"Give me a sign," he prayed to God. Then he laid out a fleece on the grass overnight. "If the grass is dry in the morning, but the fleece is wet, I shall know that it is true," he said. And so it was. But Gideon was still not satisfied, so he laid out a fleece the next night too. "If the grass is wet and the fleece is dry, I shall know for sure that you have called me," he prayed. And so it was.

Now, at last, Gideon could be certain that God had chosen him to lead the fight against the Midianites.

Gideon's Army

Judges 7:1–11

When Gideon had gathered together an army, he set up camp on a hill not far from the Midianite camp. "How few of us there are, compared to our enemy!" he worried, looking down on the vast Midianite hordes.

"Don't worry," God told Gideon. "In fact, your army is too big. Tell anyone who is afraid to go home."

"That makes sense," thought Gideon. "Frightened soldiers are no use in a battle." And so he let them go.

"Your army is still too big," said God, when He saw who was left. "Tell your men to go to the river and drink. Then send home any who put their face in the water to drink instead of cupping it in their hands."

So Gideon did as God asked. Finally, there were only 300 men left.

"I will give you victory with this army," God promised.

Gideon's heart sank at the thought of fighting the Midianites with so few men – but he trusted God. "We are ready, Lord," he said.

Gideon Defeats Midian

Judges 7:12–23

That night, Gideon gave each of his men a trumpet and a pottery jar holding a flaming light. "Tonight, we attack the enemy," he said. "At my signal, blow your trumpet, then break the jar. Make as much noise as you can!" That's exactly what they did.

As the Midianites lay sleeping, Gideon and his army crept up. "NOW!" ordered Gideon – and the night was filled with a sudden blaze of light and a terrible noise. The Midianites were terrified! Some were so confused they even attacked each other.

"A sword for the Lord and for Gideon!" yelled the Israelites, as their enemy took to their heels and fled. And so, with God's help, Gideon and his 300 men won a great victory.

Naomi's Sadness

Ruth 1

There came a time when Israel suffered a terrible famine. Soon, many people were starving, including a man called Elimelech, who lived in Bethlehem with his wife Naomi and their two sons.

"We must move to the land of Moab until the famine is over," Elimelech told his family. So they left their home far behind.

While they were living in Moab, Elimelech died, but his sons grew up there and married two Moabite girls, Orpah and Ruth. Some years later though, both the sons died too.

Naomi was very sad. "The time has come for me to return home," she said.

Orpah and Ruth decided to go with her, but when they reached Moab's border Naomi turned to them.

"Go back," she urged. "You belong with your own people."

Reluctantly, Orpah agreed, but Ruth refused.

"I'm coming with you," she told Naomi. "From now on, your people will be my people; your God will be my God."

Ruth Meets Boaz

Ruth 2

Naomi and Ruth continued together on their journey. The girl's company was a comfort to the older woman, but it did not stop her worrying. How would they live without a husband to look after them? In those days women could not earn money.

When they finally reached Bethlehem, the two women were exhausted and very hungry. Luckily, it was harvest time, and Ruth had a plan.

"Let me go out into the fields," she told Naomi. "I can pick up any grains of wheat that have been dropped. If I work hard, I can collect enough to feed us."

And that's just what she did – in a field belonging to a man called Boaz.

Boaz Marries Ruth

Ruth 3, 4

Now Boaz was Naomi's relative, and when he discovered who Ruth was, he wanted to help her. "You are welcome to work in my fields any time," he told her.

Ruth rushed to tell Naomi what had happened.

"Boaz was very kind!" she told the older woman. "He even left me extra grain to pick up."

Naomi was delighted.

"God guided you to that field!" she cried.

Of course, Naomi wanted to find a husband for Ruth – a good man who would look after them both. And she knew that Boaz was a good man. In Israel at that time, if a man died, the closest relative would take care of his family. Naomi hoped that Boaz would claim this right, so she sent Ruth to ask for his help.

Boaz was very pleased when Ruth asked for his protection. He knew how hard she worked, and he admired her kindness to Naomi.

"Take this gift as a mark of my respect," he said, presenting Ruth with a sack of grain. "I would very much like to marry you, but there is another man living in the town who is a closer relative of Naomi. We must ask him first whether he minds."

Boaz set out at once to find out.

"I already have a wife and family," the relative told him. "I'm happy for you to wed Ruth."

So Ruth and Boaz were married. Naomi was overjoyed, especially when Ruth gave birth to her first child. Little did anyone know then that Ruth – who had trusted God and helped her mother-in-law – would become the great-grandmother of Israel's greatest king – King David.

The Birth of Samuel

1 Samuel 1:1–20

Elkanah, who lived near Jerusalem, had two wives. One of them had children, but the other, called Hannah, did not. Poor Hannah! She longed for a baby, and tried her best to wait patiently for God to bless her – but one day, she could bear it no more. She fell to her knees in the Temple and poured out her feelings to God.

"Please do not forget me," she sobbed. "If you give me a son, I promise he will serve you all his life."

She didn't know that a priest called Eli was watching her.

"Whatever is the matter?" he asked her. "Are you ill?"

"No!" replied Hannah. "I am sad because I do not have a child of my own."

When Eli heard this, he was filled with pity. "May God give you the child you long for," he said kindly.

Some time later, God answered Hannah's prayers and she had a baby boy.

"I shall call our son Samuel," she told her husband, "which means 'God hears'."

The Dedication of Samuel

1 Samuel 1:21–28

When Samuel was old enough, Hannah kept her promise to God and took her child to see the priest Eli.

"This is the son God gave me," she told him. "Now I am giving him back to God. Please will you take him and look after him?"

So, from that day onwards Samuel lived in the Temple, serving God, helping Eli and learning to become a priest.

God gave Hannah more children, but she never stopped loving or missing her first-born child, Samuel. She thought about him all the time. Every year she made him new clothes and took them to the Temple. And every time that Hannah visited her son, she saw that he had grown not only in size, but also in wisdom. How proud she was! She knew that God had chosen Samuel to be His special servant.

The Calling of Samuel

1 Samuel 3

The priest Eli had two sons who also served in the Temple – but they did not love or respect God as Samuel did, and often behaved very badly. Luckily, Eli could rely on Samuel.

One night when Samuel was still young, he was sleeping in his usual place in the Temple when he was woken by the sound of someone calling his name.

"Eli must need me," thought Samuel, leaping out of bed and going to the old man.

Eli was surprised to see him. "I didn't call you, child," he said. "Go back to bed."

So Samuel lay back down and closed his eyes. Just as he was drifting off, he heard the voice once more: "Samuel!" it called.

Once again Samuel got up and ran to Eli. But again, Eli shook his head. "I didn't call," he said. "You must be dreaming."

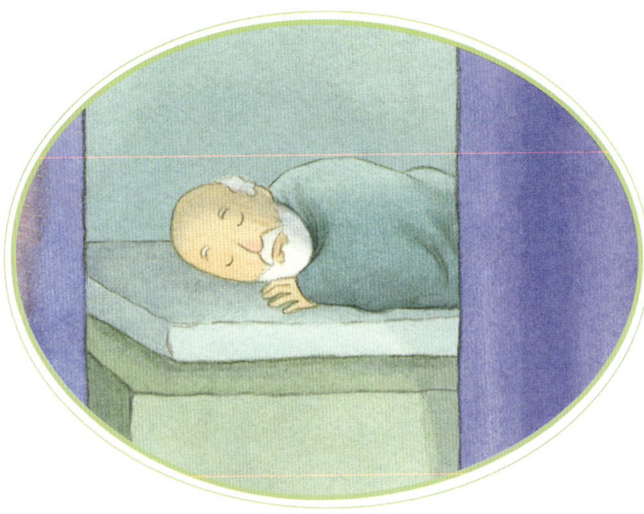

Samuel returned to his bed and tried to go to sleep, but he heard the voice calling a third time. He knew he wasn't dreaming, so he went to Eli once again.

This time, the old man realized that something important was happening. "I think God is calling to you," he told the boy. "Go back to bed now, but if you hear Him calling your name again, tell the Lord that you are ready to listen. I believe He has a message for you."

Samuel went back to bed, and the voice called his name again.

"I'm listening, Lord," cried the boy.

Then God spoke to Samuel. He explained how angry He was with Eli's sons. "I will no longer allow them to serve in the Temple," He announced. "They are not fit to be priests."

In the morning, Samuel was afraid to tell Eli what God had said. But the old man told him to be brave and truthful. So Samuel repeated God's message.

"You were right to tell me," said Eli. "God knows what is best for all of us, even if it is not what we want to hear."

Samson's Birth

Judges 13

A long time passed, and once again the Israelites forgot about God and went back to the old ways, praying to other gods. God was angry that they had forgotten about Him. As a punishment, He allowed the Philistines to rule over the Israelites for forty years. Times were very hard.

An Israelite called Manoah and his wife longed for God to send them a new leader to rule their nation and, even more than that, they longed to have a child of their own. One day, God sent an angel to Manoah. The angel told him that he and his wife would have a son, who would help protect the Israelites from their enemies. When the boy was born, he was called Samson. As a sign that Samson belonged to God, his parents never cut his hair.

Samson grew up to be very strong, with long, dark hair. He was so strong that he even killed a lion with his bare hands!

Samson and Delilah

Judges 16:4–22

From then on, Samson knew that God wanted him to use his amazing strength against the Philistines. And that is what he did. He destroyed their crops and, once, killed a thousand of them using only a donkey's jawbone as a weapon! When the Philistines tried to capture Samson, he always got away. But the Philistines were determined to get their revenge on him.

Their chance soon came. Samson had fallen in love with a beautiful Philistine girl, called Delilah. When the five Philistine kings heard this, they offered her lots of money if she could make Samson tell her the secret of his strength. Delilah agreed.

"What makes you so strong?" she asked. "Could anyone ever tie you up?"

"If you tie me up with new bowstrings, I'll be as weak as anybody else," he laughed. Then another time, "Use brand new rope to tie me up… weave my hair into a loom…" Every time she asked, Samson gave her a different answer.

Delilah tried everything that Samson told her, but nothing she did weakened him.

Delilah nagged Samson to tell her the truth. “If you won’t tell me, you don’t really love me,” she said.

But Samson did love Delilah and in the end he told her his secret. “My hair is a sign that I belong to God. I would lose all my strength if it were cut.”

Delilah waited for Samson to fall asleep that night, and then summoned a man to cut off his hair. Immediately, Samson lost all his strength. The Philistines came and took him prisoner.

Samson was blinded, chained and taken to a prison in Gaza. He was made to work very hard. But gradually Samson’s hair grew back again.

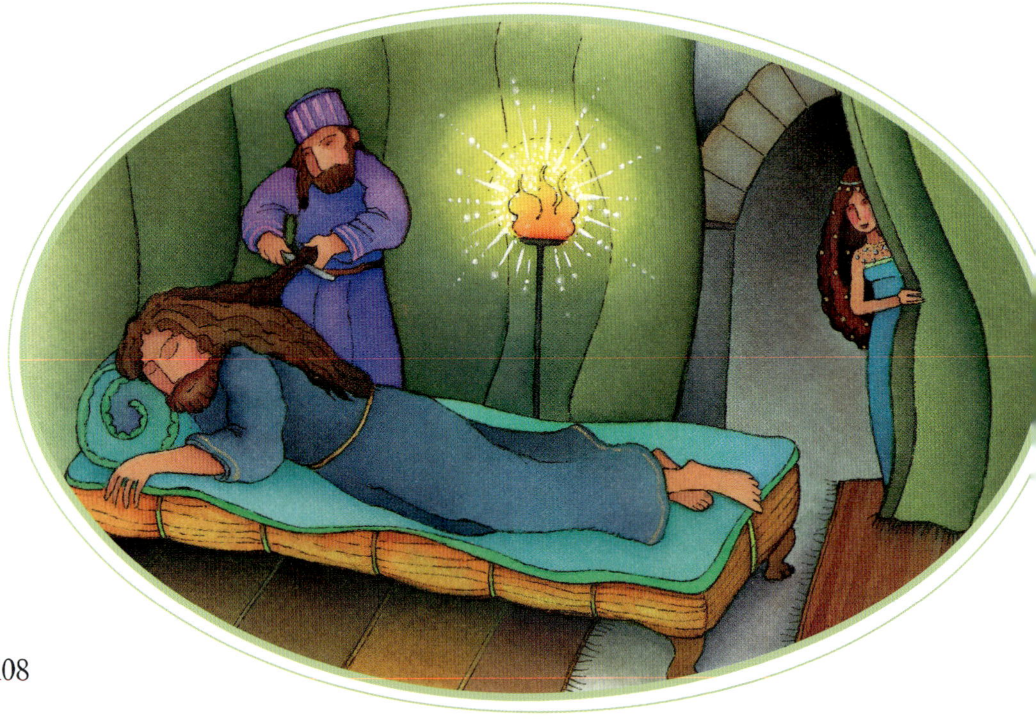

Samson Destroys the Temple

Judges 16:23–30

One day, the Philistines held a feast in honour of Dagon, their god. They brought Samson from the prison to their temple. The temple was crowded with people, and they were all laughing at him and mocking him. Samson prayed to God to give him strength. Then he reached out and pushed against the two pillars supporting the temple. He pushed with all his might, and suddenly the temple collapsed. Everyone inside was killed.

Samson had been the leader of his people for twenty years. The destruction of the Philistines' temple was his last act against the enemies of Israel.

The Ark is Captured and Returned

1 Samuel 4, 5, 6

Once again, the Israelites were at war with the Philistines. This time, the Israelites were losing the battle. They decided to take the Ark, the special box containing God's laws, into battle with them. They thought that this would protect them from the Philistines.

The two sons of Eli, the old priest, brought the Ark to the front line of the battle.

But then a terrible thing happened. The Philistines won the battle and captured the Ark. They took it back to their city, Ashdod, and took the Ark into the temple of Dagon, the false god they worshipped.

The next morning, when the priests of Dagon went into the temple, they saw the statue of their god lying flat on its face in front of the Ark. They were frightened.

The priests of Dagon lifted the idol up and put it back into its place. But the next morning it was on the ground in front of the Ark again. This time though, the statue had been smashed into pieces.

After this, the people of Ashdod all developed horrible diseases.

The Philistines decided to move the Ark to another city. But horrible diseases broke out among the people there too, and into the next city where the Ark was taken.

The Philistines decided they had had enough. They called all their priests and wise men and asked what to do.

"You must send the box back to the Israelites," said the wise men. "You should send a gift for their God as well."

So the Philistines sent the Ark and their gifts back to a village called Beth Shemesh, where Joshua had lived. The Ark was placed on a large rock in the middle of a field that had belonged to Joshua and all the Israelite people rejoiced.

Israel Asks God for a King

1 Samuel 8

Samuel was a good, fair king. He loved God and he loved the good, honest way of life of his people. But Samuel's two sons were not like him at all. They were greedy and only interested in money. The Israelites did not want either of Samuel's sons to lead them when Samuel died. "We need a king," thcy told Samuel. This made Samuel unhappy. God was the only true leader. Samuel didn't know what to do.

He prayed to God for help. God told Samuel to tell the people what a king would be like.

"He will make your sons fight in his armies," said Samuel. "He will force you to work the land for him and he will take the best crops. You will become his slaves." But the people didn't listen.

"We want a king," they insisted.

When Samuel told God that the Israelites wouldn't change their minds, God told Samuel to give them what they wanted. "Give them their king," He said.

Saul Meets Samuel

1 Samuel 9

There was a very handsome young man called Saul whose father's donkeys had run away. Saul and a young servant boy went into the hills to look for them.

They walked a long way, searching and searching for the donkeys. It began to grow late. "Let's go home," Saul said. "Soon my father will stop worrying about the donkeys and start to worry about us."

But the boy said, "I have heard there is a prophet, a wise man of God, in the town over there. Let's go and ask him if he can help us."

As they went down into the town, Samuel the prophet was coming towards them.

Samuel was not in the least surprised to meet Saul because God had already told him the exact time and place where he would meet the man God had chosen to be Israel's king.

Samuel invited Saul and his servant back to his home for a fine meal.

Samuel Anoints Saul

1 Samuel 10

The next day at dawn, Saul and the boy set off for home and Samuel walked part of the way with them. "The donkeys have been found," Samuel told Saul. "Your father has stopped worrying about them and is worrying about you."

When they were away from the town, Samuel told the boy to go on ahead. Then he told Saul that God had chosen him to be the first king of Israel.

Saul was astonished, but Samuel told him he could trust God.

Then Saul knelt down and Samuel poured oil on Saul's head as a sign that God had chosen him to be king.

Saul's Mistakes

1 Samuel 13:1–14; 14:24–46

At the beginning, Saul was a good king, but sadly that did not last. Saul became proud. He began to think less of God and more of himself. When he won battles, he thought it was because he was clever, and not because God helped him.

Saul did what he wanted and not what God wanted. He disobeyed God and would not listen to Samuel.

Saul fought many battles against the Philistines and Israel's other enemies.

By now he had become so stubborn that in the middle of one battle, he decided none of his soldiers should eat anything until the battle was won. He sent out an order saying that anyone who ate anything would be killed. But not everyone heard this order.

Saul's son Jonathan was leading a group of soldiers on the battlefield. They were all very hungry because they had not eaten all day. Then Jonathan found a honeycomb, full of wild honey. He dipped a stick into the honeycomb and ate some of the honey. The men with him were horrified. "Didn't you hear the king's command?" they asked. "Anyone who eats before the battle is over must be put to death."

Because Saul was so proud he felt he should keep his word and have his son killed. But the people loved Jonathan and stood up to Saul. Jonathan's life was spared.

But Saul continued to be proud and angry. He did not make time for God and refused to listen to anything Samuel had to say to him.

Saul is Rejected as King

1 Samuel 15

Saul continued to fight battles against Israel's enemies. But when he won victories he was not interested in obeying God – all he wanted was to get as much for himself as possible.

God was very sad that His chosen king was behaving so badly and decided he should not be king any more. God told Samuel that Saul was no longer fit to rule the people of Israel and he must find a new king.

Samuel prayed all night asking God to tell him what to do, and God told him to go to Bethlehem where he would find the man He had chosen to be Israel's next king.

David is Chosen as the New King

1 Samuel 16:1–13

God told Samuel to go to the home of a man called Jesse, who lived in Bethlehem. God had chosen one of Jesse's sons to become the next king.

When Samuel arrived at Jesse's home, all the sons came in to share a meal. Samuel spoke to each son in turn. Each time he thought, "Surely this must be the chosen one." But each time God said, "No. It is not important what a person looks like. What matters is what they are like inside."

One by one, God rejected the seven sons in front of Samuel. Samuel was puzzled. He asked Jesse if he had any more sons.

"Yes," said Jesse. "There is the youngest, David. He is out in the fields looking after the sheep."

Samuel asked Jesse to send for David. As soon as the boy walked in, God said to Samuel, "This is the chosen one!"

Samuel poured oil on David's head to show that God had chosen him to be king.

After Samuel had gone, David continued to look after his father's sheep. Wild animals often attacked the flock. David learned to be skilful with a catapult to scare away hungry bears and lions.

God loved David, and was always with him.

David Plays for Saul

1 Samuel 16:14–23

David was clever in other ways too. He loved music and singing, and he played the harp beautifully. News of his skills spread far across the land.

Meanwhile, Saul was becoming more and more distant from God. He had terrible moods, and an evil spirit tormented him. Worse still, Samuel no longer visited him at his palace.

One of Saul's attendants thought that soothing harp music might calm the king. David was sent for and, whenever he played the harp for Saul, the king became calmer and happier. Once the king felt better, David planned to return home.

But then there came some worrying news. The battle with the Philistines was not going well. The Philistines had a champion, a huge and fierce warrior called Goliath. He was about three metres tall, and much stronger than any ox.

David Defeats Goliath

1 Samuel 17; 18:1–9

Goliath strutted up and down, challenging the Israelites to fight.

"Where's the champion of Israel?" he shouted. "Send him to fight me! If he kills me, we will be your slaves. If I kill him, you will be ours."

No one stepped forward to take up Goliath's challenge. They were all too scared.

One day, when David was taking food to his brothers in the army, he heard Goliath's taunts. "Who is he to challenge the army of the living God?" asked David. "I will fight him."

Saul heard about David's offer and sent for him.

"I have to fight lions and bears to keep my father's sheep safe," David told him. "If God can protect me from wild animals, he will protect me now."

At last, Saul agreed to David's request. He gave him his own armour and sword, but it was too heavy for David. "I will fight him with what I am used to," David said. He took off the armour, picked up his sling and set off to meet Goliath.

When Goliath saw David coming towards him, he laughed. "What sort of champion is this?" he sneered.

"I come in the name of the God of Israel," replied David. "He is a stronger champion than you!"

David took a stone from his bag, placed it into his sling and took aim. The stone hurtled towards Goliath. It struck him on the forehead and broke his skull. Goliath fell down dead.

The Philistines were afraid and ran into the hills. The Israelites had won.

After the victory, the Israelites were very happy. But Saul was jealous. He could see that everyone loved David. Saul sat in his palace thinking of ways he could harm David.

David Escapes from Saul

1 Samuel 19, 20

One of Saul's daughters, Michal, fell in love with David. Saul was happy for David to marry her, but he was happy for the wrong reasons. He thought that if David was a member of his family, it would be easier to harm him.

David went back into battle and won many victories for the Israelites. But Saul continued to plot against him. Michal was very worried.

One night, after David had returned from battle, Michal warned him that he was in danger from Saul and must go away. She helped him to escape from the palace through a window. Then she laid a statue on David's bed and threw a cover over it so that Saul's men would not know he had gone. This gave David more time to escape to safety.

David Sings

Psalm 56

David was sad that Saul had turned against him. He felt very alone. But he remembered that God was always with him, and he sang a special hymn (called a psalm) as a way of talking to God.

Be with me O God,
I am alone and trampled on by my enemies.
Many people have turned against me.
But I put my trust in You, Lord,
You are always with me.

O God, I praise your word,
I trust You to take care of me,
With You beside me I am not afraid.

Thank You God, for keeping me safe,
For delivering me from death.
You have kept my feet from stumbling
So I can walk with You in the light of life.

Thank You God, that You are always with me.

Amen.

David Spares Saul

1 Samuel 26

As time passed, more and more of the Israelite people wanted to follow David, not Saul. Saul became more and more angry.

Saul was determined to find David and kill him. He went out into the far hills with a group of soldiers to hunt David down. When darkness fell, they made a camp for the night and Saul fell asleep in a cave.

This was where David and his men found Saul, fast asleep. "You can kill your enemy now," said David's followers. "Then you won't have to keep running from his anger."

But David said, "I cannot kill the King of Israel," and turned to leave the cave. He left a sign to show he had been there, though. He and his men took Saul's spear and water jar. Then, when they were a safe distance away from the camp, David gave a great shout to wake Saul's guards. He wanted them to know how easily he could have killed the king if he had wanted to.

Saul Dies and David Mourns

2 Samuel 1

When Saul realized that David had been close enough to kill him but had spared his life he was ashamed. But he and David remained enemies.

Saul was no longer a strong and powerful king. Soon afterwards there was another terrible battle against the Philistines. Knowing that he was defeated, Saul took his own life with his sword. Saul's son Jonathan, who had been David's true friend, was killed in battle.

Even though their friendship had ended badly, David was sad that Saul had died in such a way. He was even sadder about his good friend Jonathan. David wrote a song of lament for the two men. "How the mighty have fallen," he sang. "Saul and Jonathan, such wonderful men. In death they were not divided."

David was now determined to become king.

David Becomes King

2 Samuel 5:1–7

After Saul died, David's wish came true and he became King of Israel. But life was not going to be easy for him. People who had supported Saul did not support David.

The Philistines, too, were always waiting for a chance to return to the country.

More than anything, David wanted to conquer the city of Jerusalem, so that he could take the Ark, the sacred box of God's laws, there.

When, at last, David did capture the city of Jerusalem, the people celebrated with music and dancing. There were wonderful feasts, and gifts were offered to God.

Best of all, David made Jerusalem God's city and he set about building a royal palace there.

David's Plans for the Temple

2 Samuel 7; 1 Chronicles 17

Now that David was king, he had a fine palace. Then he realized that, although he had a wonderful place to live, God's special book of laws, the Ark, was still living in a tent. This didn't seem right.

That very night, God spoke to a man called Nathan in a dream. Nathan was a holy man, a prophet, living in David's court. "I am tired of living in a tent," God said. "Go and tell David the king to build me a fine house of cedar wood."

Nathan and David both thought that building a temple for God was a good idea. They drew up plans to make sure that everything would be just as God wanted it.

But then David started to enjoy being king and all the wealth and power that came with it. He forgot how much God had done for him. He stopped listening to God and behaved in ways that made God angry.

The prophet Nathan saw what was happening and told David that he had done wrong. He gave David a message. God had decided that it would be David's son, not David himself, who would complete the building of the Temple.

David was very sad about this. He said sorry to God. Then he carried on working on the plans, and writing hymns to be sung in the Temple one day, after his son became king.

David Sings

Psalm 24

Here is one of the hymns that David wrote.

The Earth is the Lord God's and everything in it,
Everything on Earth belongs to God.
God has created land, and sky and water.
Everything created belongs to God.

All who love the Lord God, and seek to be near Him
Will receive His blessing and protection.
The God of Jacob is great and glorious.
He is the King of Glory.

Open up you gates of the city,
You doors of the temple,
Be open for the King of Glory to come in.

The Lord God is strong and mighty,
He gives us victory in battle,
He protects us from our enemies.
He is the King of Glory.

The Lord our God is almighty,
He is the King of Glory.
Open up you gates of the city,
Be open for the King of Glory to come in.

David and Mephibosheth

2 Samuel 9

Now that David was a great king, he wanted to do something for the family of his friend Jonathan. He asked his servants if any of Jonathan's children were still alive.

One of the servants said: "Jonathan's son is still alive. He is called Mephibosheth, and he is frail and lame."

David was very glad to hear that Jonathan's son – Saul's grandson – was still alive. He asked that the young man be brought to see him. Mephibosheth was given a seat at the king's own banqueting table, and David himself waited on him. Then he told Mephibosheth that because he was the son of his loyal friend Jonathan, he would be given all the lands that had belonged to Saul. And there would always be a place for Mephibosheth at the king's table.

Solomon Becomes King

1 Kings 1:28–3:15

Before King David died, he spoke to his son Solomon who would be king after him. He told Solomon to be a strong king, to trust in God and to follow His commands. "Then God will keep His promise that my descendants will rule this nation," he said.

When Solomon became king, he was determined to be a powerful and just ruler so he sent away all his father's old enemies. He set about organizing his kingdom with great care.

One night, Solomon had a dream. He dreamed that God asked him, "What do you need from me?"

Solomon thought carefully and replied, "I am very young to rule over so many people. Please give me wisdom to make the right and true decisions."

This answer pleased God, and He gave Solomon more wisdom and understanding than anyone had ever had before.

Solomon's Wisdom

1 Kings 3; 2 Chronicles 1

Solomon became famous for his wisdom, but he never forgot that it was a gift from God.

One day, two women asked Solomon to judge who was the real mother of a baby. Solomon thought and thought. Then he suggested that the baby should be cut in half, so that the women could have half each and share the baby between them. The false mother agreed straight away, but the real mother was horrified. "No," she said, "I would rather my baby lived with someone else than was killed."

At once Solomon knew who the real mother was.

Because King Solomon was a wise ruler who trusted God, he made good decisions and his people lived in peace.

Solomon Builds the Temple

1 Kings 5–8

In the fourth year of his reign, King Solomon started to build a magnificent temple for God. The foundations and the walls of the Temple were built from beautiful large stones and cedar wood from the forests of Lebanon.

The Temple took seven years to build, but at long last it was finished. It was beautiful. Outside there were courtyards, where people could offer God their gifts. Inside at the back was a windowless square, with floors and walls covered in gold. This innermost room was to hold the Ark, the special box which contained God's laws. It was decorated with carved figures of winged creatures, palm trees and flowers, all covered in gold. The outer room gleamed with gold too.

The Dedication of the Temple

2 Chronicles 7:1–10

Solomon decided to hold a special ceremony to show that the Temple was for God. The priests made offerings and the Ark, the special box containing God's laws, was carried from its tent into the Temple's innermost room. At that moment, the Temple was filled with a dazzling light, the light of God's presence.

King Solomon prayed: "Lord, God of Israel, hear the prayers of your people. Listen to them and help them always."

Then Solomon turned to the people. "You must be true to God. You must obey His commands," he said.

When the ceremony was over, a great feast was held. The celebrations lasted for a whole week.

Solomon Writes Lots of Wise Sayings, Called Proverbs

Proverbs 1–3, 6

Solomon didn't only speak wise words, he wrote a lot of wise sayings down in a book, the Book of Proverbs.

"The fear of God is the beginning of knowledge," he wrote. And: "Only fools despise wisdom and learning."

Solomon wrote that wisdom was better than gold or precious jewels. He told children to listen to what their fathers and mothers told them, and not to listen to the words of bad people. "Do not forget loyalty and faithfulness," he told them. "Wear them like a necklace. Write them on your heart."

As well as advice like this, Solomon's book included a lot of wise sayings about how to behave. Parents read the book to their children to teach them right from wrong.

Solomon also told stories about plants and flowers, insects and animals, to teach people how to live good and useful lives.

Here is one of the stories.

Don't be lazy. Look at how hard the ants work in summer. They store up food for the winter. But if you are lazy and lie around sleeping while times are good, poverty will creep up on you while you are not looking.

The Book of Proverbs also tells of the importance of loving God and obeying His laws. "Trust in the Lord with all your heart," says Solomon. "Acknowledge that all your wisdom comes from Him."

The Queen of Sheba Visits Solomon

1 Kings 10:1–13; 11:31–32; 2 Chronicles 9:1–12

Stories of Solomon's wisdom spread far and wide across the world to other lands. Soon the stories reached the land of Sheba.

When the Queen of Sheba heard about Solomon, she decided to see for herself how wise he was. She thought up a list of very difficult questions; questions that only the wisest of men could answer. Then she packed her finest jewels, gold and spices and she set out for Jerusalem.

Everyone stopped to look as the queen entered Jerusalem.

The queen went to see Solomon. She asked all her questions, and Solomon answered them easily.

Then the queen knew that Solomon was indeed a wise man.

"I can see that God has given His people a wise king because He loves them so much," she said.

The queen was right about this. Israel was rich and peaceful for much of Solomon's reign. He built many beautiful palaces, and great cities grew. But sadly the good times did not last. Solomon became too fond of spending money on fine things. He needed more and more gold to pay for all his grand projects. He made the Israelites pay lots of taxes and he forced thousands of men to work on his buildings. Many of his people became poor and unhappy while Solomon was king.

Worse than this, Solomon began to forget God and His goodness. He did not remain faithful to God, as his father David had. This made God sad. God spoke to Solomon.

"The kingdom of Israel will be taken from your son, since you have not followed my commands," He said. And as time passed, God's words came true. Some bad kings came after Solomon.

Ahab and Jezebel

1 Kings 16:29–34; 1 Kings 21

When King Solomon died, Israel was split into two kingdoms. The people from Judah in the south followed Solomon's son, Rehoboam. But Jeroboam, the son of Nebat, became ruler of the north.

The kings of the north who came after Jeroboam were not faithful to God. One of them, Ahab, married a woman called Jezebel from another tribe. She worshipped a false god. It soon became clear that the real ruler was not Ahab at all – it was Jezebel!

Ahab and Jezebel were cruel and selfish. One day, Ahab saw a man called Naboth working in a beautiful vineyard, next door to his palace.

"Will you sell me your land?" he asked. "It is just what I want for my vegetable garden."

"I'm sorry," replied Naboth humbly. "I can't do that. This vineyard has belonged to my family for many years. It is only fair that my children and their children will have it in time."

Now, Ahab was not used to people refusing him, and he was very angry. "How dare you say no?" he shrieked. Queen Jezebel was furious too.

It wasn't long before Jezebel found a way to get what she wanted. She hatched a wicked plan to get Naboth into trouble, and had him put to death for treason.

"That's how to deal with these people!" she laughed cruelly, as she handed Ahab the documents that made him the new owner of the vineyard.

Soon, everyone in the land was afraid of Ahab and Jezebel. They knew that if they did not do as the king and queen commanded, there would be trouble.

Elijah Stops the Rain

1 Kings 17:1–6

Queen Jezebel was determined that everyone in the kingdom should worship her god, Baal. So she gave the order for all of God's prophets to be killed. "Everyone will soon forget about Israel's God and His laws," she sneered.

But God wasn't going to let that happen. He chose a man called Elijah to help bring His people back to worship Him.

Elijah went to speak to Ahab and Jezebel. "There will be no rain in Israel until my God says so," he told them. And so it was.

No rain fell for two years, no matter how hard the king and queen prayed to Baal. Soon the land was parched and people were starving. Ahab and Jezebel were furious with Elijah, and wanted to kill him, but God knew what they were up to.

He told Elijah to hide in a secret place, and even sent ravens to bring him food to eat.

Elijah and the Widow

1 Kings 17:7–16

One day, God told Elijah to go to a certain town. "A widow there will give you food and drink," he said.

It was a long journey, and by the time Elijah arrived he was very hungry – but he knew that God would not fail him. And he was right. There at the gates, he met a widow.

"Will you give me some food?" asked Elijah.

"I'm sorry," the woman replied. "There is a drought here – I have only enough for one last meal."

"Don't worry," Elijah answered. "God will provide."

And so he did. Every day, there was enough food in the pot to feed the widow's family – and Elijah too – for as long as the drought lasted.

Elijah and the Prophets of Baal

1 Kings 18:1–40

At last, God sent Elijah back to King Ahab. "It has not rained for three years!" thundered the king, when he saw Elijah. "It is all your fault!"

"It is not my fault, but your own," replied Elijah calmly. "You have turned your back on the one true God." Then he told Ahab to bring his people and the prophets of Baal to Mount Carmel.

King Ahab did as Elijah asked. Soon, a huge crowd had gathered.

"It is time to see who is the one true God," announced Elijah. "I challenge the prophets of Baal. They must offer a bull to their god and I will offer one to mine. The one true God will be the one who sends a fire to burn the offering."

The priests of Baal set to work. They made an altar and laid a bull on it. Then they prayed for their god to send fire. "Baal, answer us!" they cried, but no one answered. Nothing happened.

Next, it was Elijah's turn. He built his altar and dug a ditch around it, then he placed his bull on a stack of firewood. He said to the people, "Fill four large jars with water and pour it over the bull and the firewood."

He told them to do it again and again until the water ran down the altar and filled the ditch.

Everyone was amazed. "Surely all that water will put out any flames!" they cried. "He must be mad!"

Very calmly, Elijah began to pray. At once, God sent down fire and, even though the wood was soaked, the offering burst into flames.

The Return of the Rain

1 Kings 18:41–46

At last, the crowds on Mount Carmel knew the truth. "Elijah's God is the one true God," they cried.

Then Elijah spoke. "Take the prophets of Baal away!" he ordered. "Let the wicked worship of this other god end today."

He looked up to the heavens and began to pray. At once, the wind rose, the skies darkened and heavy rain began to fall for the first time in years.

"What must I do now?" asked King Ahab, shaken by what he had seen.

"Go home," replied Elijah, "and tell others what you have learned today. There is only one true God."

Elijah Runs Away

1 Kings 19:1–9

When Ahab told Jezebel what had happened, she was furious. "Elijah can't get away with this! I will have him killed!" she cried.

Of course, it wasn't long before Elijah heard of the queen's threat – and his heart sank. "How can I reason with a woman like that?" he thought. So he ran away into the desert to hide.

As he tramped along, Elijah felt more and more hopeless. "What's the use of even trying?" he thought. At last, hungry and exhausted, he lay down under a tree and fell asleep. Then God sent an angel to take care of him.

Elijah was woken by a voice. "Come, Elijah," it said. "You must eat." Elijah sat up and looked about. There beside him was some bread and water – a gift from God.

The Still, Small Voice

1 Kings 19:10–18

Elijah began to feel better. He knew now that God was watching over him. Soon he felt strong enough to continue with his journey.

Elijah walked for forty days and nights and eventually arrived at Mount Sinai. He found a cave to shelter in. Then he waited for God to find him. And God did.

"What are you doing here, Elijah?" He asked.

Although Elijah had won over the people on Mount Carmel he still felt discouraged. "The Israelites have torn down your altars and killed your prophets. I am the only one left!" he cried.

Just then, a great wind blew up, as powerful as the turmoil that Elijah felt inside. Rocks tumbled off the mountainside as the ground shook, and flames shot into the sky.

At last, there was silence. Everything was calm again.

In the silence, Elijah heard a whisper. He pulled his cloak around him and went and stood at the entrance to the cave. Then God spoke in a quiet voice. “Why are you here?” he said.

“I am the only one left,” repeated Elijah. “And now Jezebel wants to kill me too.”

“You are not alone,” God reassured him. “Go back the way you came. There are still thousands of my followers in Israel who have never worshipped Baal. Find a man named Elisha.

He will help you carry out my work. Leave Ahab and Jezebel to me – I will deal with them.”

Elijah felt much better when he heard these words. He knew that God was looking after him and that he would no longer have to carry on God’s work all by himself.

Elijah and Elisha

1 Kings 19:19–21

Elijah went in search of Elisha, just as God had instructed. Finally, he found him working in his father's fields, ploughing the earth with a team of oxen.

"God has chosen you for a very special task," he told him. "You must come with me, and learn to be God's prophet."

Now, Elisha belonged to a wealthy family, but as soon as he heard what Elijah had to say, he followed the old man. "It is God's will," he said. "Let me first kiss my father and mother goodbye, then I will come with you."

Elijah was overjoyed. He was growing older every day and getting tired. Elisha would be a huge comfort to him in his work.

Elijah is Taken up to Heaven

2 Kings 2:1–18

Elijah and Elisha worked very happily together for God. The old man was a wise teacher, and Elisha was proud to learn from him. But eventually Elijah knew that he must hand over all his work to the young man. "It is time for me to leave you!" he told him. "If you see me when I am taken it is a sign that you will take my place."

As he spoke, a gust of wind lifted Elijah into the clouds.

"Don't go, master!" cried Elisha, but he saw that Elijah had been taken up to heaven. Sadly, Elisha picked up the old man's cloak.

"I must put on the cloak now," he told himself. "I must continue where Elijah left off."

The Widow and the Oil

2 Kings 4:1–7

Some time later, a widow came to Elisha for help. Her husband had been one of Elijah's followers.

"My husband was faithful to God, but he borrowed money from a bad man," she said. "Now the moneylender wants to take my sons away as slaves."

"What do you have in your house?" Elisha asked.

"Only a small jar of olive oil," the woman replied.

Elisha told her to ask her neighbours for empty jars.

"Get as many as you can," he said. "Then go home with your sons and fill each jar with oil."

The woman's sons brought the jars to her one by one. She kept pouring oil into them from the small jar, until all the jars were full. Then the oil stopped flowing.

The woman told Elisha what had happened.

"Sell the oil and pay back the money you owe," said Elisha. "You and your sons can live on the money that's left over."

The Shunammite Woman

2 Kings 4:8–37

Elisha had a friend who was always kind to him when he visited the town of Shunem. She had a son who she loved very much. But one day, while the boy was helping his father in the fields, he started to feel ill.

"My head hurts!" he cried.

His father sent him home, but a few hours later the boy died. In grief, the Shunammite woman laid the boy on a bed and went to find Elisha.

When Elisha arrived the woman showed him to the room where the boy lay dead. Elisha prayed to God to bring the child back to life. God told Elisha what to do.

Elisha lay down and put his mouth to the child's mouth. The boy started to breathe! His body grew warm and he sneezed seven times. Then he opened his eyes.

Elisha called the Shunammite woman.

"Your son is alive!" he said. "Rejoice!"

The Healing of Naaman

2 Kings 5

Naaman was the commander of the king's army in Syria. He was very rich and important, but he had a terrible disease called leprosy. Even with all his riches, he couldn't cure his illness.

One of his wife's servants was an Israelite girl, and she told them about Elisha.

"He is God's prophet," she said. "He could cure the master."

So Naaman went to Israel with lots of money, horses and chariots. But when he arrived at Elisha's house, Elisha sent his servant out.

"My master says you must wash yourself in the Jordan River seven times," said the servant. "Your skin will be healed."

But Naaman was a proud man, and he felt angry. He thought that Elisha should treat him with more respect and do something more exciting then just telling him to bathe in a river.

"Elisha should have come to me himself," he said. "The rivers in Syria are better than the rivers in Israel. I could just as well wash in them and be cured!"

He wanted to go home, but his servants persuaded him to do what Elisha had said. So Naaman went to the river and dipped himself in the water seven times. When he came out, his skin was clear and he was healed!

Naaman rushed back to see Elisha. He tried to offer him gifts, but Elisha refused to take them.

"Now I know that your Lord is the only true God," Naaman said.

"Go in peace," said Elisha.

The Kings of Judah

2 Kings 16–22

The tribes of Israel disagreed about who should rule the followers of Moses. The northern group became the Kingdom of Israel. The southern group formed the Kingdom of Judah. Its capital was Jerusalem.

Both kingdoms were meant to keep to the religion of Moses. But Judah had the most holy city, with its great Temple. Even so, some of its kings turned their back on Jewish beliefs. They built statues and temples to many gods, instead of to the One True God. The Bible calls these rulers 'bad kings'.

All the kings of Israel were bad and so were many of the kings of Judah. Uzziah was one of the better kings and so was his son Jotham. But the next king, Ahaz, was bad. He brought statues of other gods to the ancient Temple and he ignored the words of God's prophets.

Ahaz's son, Hezekiah, hated the way his father

had lived. As soon as he became king, he ordered the priests to repair and clean the Temple. The job took sixteen days.

God was happy with Hezekiah. He protected him and the people of Judah from the powerful Assyrian army who wanted to attack them.

After Hezekiah, his twelve-year-old only son, Manasseh, became king. He was fascinated by other religions and led the people back into evil ways. Like Ahaz, he had altars built to worship Baal and other gods inside the Temple. He also killed many innocent people. Manasseh ruled for fifty-five years.

Manasseh's son, Amon, inherited the kingdom. He was just as bad as his father, but the people rebelled and killed him after only two years.

Judah was saved when Amon's eight-year-old son Josiah became king. He ruled for thirty-one years. During that time, he brought back many religious traditions that had been forgotten over the years. Some of those, like the feast of Passover, are still important Jewish holy days.

God Calls Jonah

Jonah 1:1–6

Not all prophets were willing to say "Yes" when God called them. After all, being a messenger for God could be very dangerous! One such prophet was Jonah.

One day, God told Jonah that He had a message for him to give to the people of Nineveh, the capital city of Assyria. The Assyrians were the enemies of God's people, and they were cruel and wicked.

"Tell the King and the people of Nineveh that the city will be destroyed in forty days' time," said God. "Tell them I know about their wicked ways and they must stop now!"

But Jonah didn't want to go. Instead, he ran away and got on a boat that was going to Spain. As soon as the boat set sail, he settled down to sleep on the deck.

God was angry with Jonah for disobeying Him. He sent a huge storm, and the boat pitched and tossed on the waves. The sailors cried out to their gods to save them.

Jonah carried on sleeping, unaware of what was going on, until the captain woke him. "Pray to your God to save us," he cried.

A Big Storm and a Big Fish

Jonah 1:7–17

Jonah realized that it was his fault they were caught in such a terrible storm. "Throw me into the sea!" he said. "Then the storm will calm down."

At first the captain refused, but the storm got even worse. Reluctantly, he threw Jonah overboard.

As soon as Jonah touched the water, the sea calmed and the storm died down.

As Jonah sank beneath the waves, he felt sure that he was going to drown. He called out for God to save him. God heard him, and sent a big fish to swallow him up alive.

Nineveh is Saved

Jonah 2–3

Jonah stayed inside the fish for three whole days. He was very sorry for disobeying God, and told Him so in his prayers.

God listened to Jonah's prayers. He knew that Jonah was sorry, and so He made the big fish swim to the shore and spit him out onto a beach.

Once again, God told Jonah to take his message to Nineveh. This time Jonah did as he was told. He went straight to Nineveh, and told the people that God would destroy their city if they didn't change their ways.

The people were very sorry and upset. They immediately stopped their wickedness and promised to lead better lives.

When God saw how the people had changed, He forgave them, and did not destroy their city after all.

Jonah Learns His Lesson

Jonah 4

Was Jonah pleased that the city was saved? No, he was angry. "I knew you would let them off!" he complained to God. "It's not fair. The people don't deserve it."

And, with that, Jonah went to sit outside the city in the scorching sun. He felt so miserable he wanted to die.

But God made a big, shady plant grow to protect Jonah from the fierce heat. Jonah began to feel less miserable.

The next day, God sent a little worm to nibble at the plant's roots and soon the plant died. The sun started beating down on Jonah yet again.

"I was glad of that plant," said Jonah crossly. "I'm sorry it has died. It's not fair!"

"You are sorry that this one little plant has died, but you did nothing to make it grow," said God. "How do you think I feel about the people of Nineveh – the innocent children, the animals? I gave them all life."

Now Jonah understood how much God cared for the world He had created. He was sorry too.

God Calls Isaiah to Become a Prophet

Isaiah 6

Not all God's chosen messengers ran away, however. Some answered God's call straight away and agreed to become His prophets.

When Uzziah ruled Judah he was a good king who followed God's laws, but the people he ruled did not. In the year that the king died, a man named Isaiah had a vision. In this vision, he saw God sitting upon His heavenly throne and the train of his robe filled the temple. He was surrounded by angels. The light was dazzling and all the angels sang hymns of praise to God.

Holy, Holy, Holy,
is the Lord of Heaven,
All Heaven and Earth are
full of God's glory.

At the sound of their voices the temple shook and filled with smoke.

Isaiah was very frightened. He knew he did not deserve to see such an amazing sight. "I am a sinful man," he cried. "And I live among sinful people. What can I do?"

Then one of the angels took a live coal from the heavenly altar with a pair of tongs and flew towards Isaiah. The angel touched Isaiah on the lips with the coal. It did not burn him.

The angel said, "Your guilt has gone and your sins are forgiven." With this, Isaiah was able to speak God's words and pass on God's messages.

As Isaiah stood there amazed, he heard a great voice, the voice of God Himself, saying: "Who shall I send to speak to my people? Who will be a messenger for me?"

And Isaiah said, "Here I am, Lord. Send me."

So God told Isaiah what he should say to the people of Israel. Throughout his long life, Isaiah would be God's messenger and a great prophet.

Isaiah Prophesies the Birth of the Chosen One

Isaiah 7:14; 9:6–7

Some years after this, when Ahaz was King of Judah, life became very difficult for the Israelites. Their nation was often at war and the people suffered greatly because of their king's wickedness.

Ahaz did not follow God's laws and he ignored Isaiah's repeated warnings. But God had not forgotten his people. He gave Isaiah a message of hope to pass on to them.

"A young woman will have a baby, a son," God said. "And his name shall be Immanuel, which means 'God is with us'."

A little later, God sent another message about this special baby for Isaiah to give to the people.

This is how Isaiah described what was going to happen:

The people who walked in darkness have seen a great light.
They were sad, God has made them happy.
They rejoice as people rejoice at the harvest.
A child will be born for us.
A son will be given to us.
All authority will rest on his shoulders.
He will be called Wonderful Counsellor,
Mighty God, Everlasting Father, The Prince of Peace.
He will come from the family of David, and will rule for ever.
He will bring peace to the nations.
There will be peace forever in his name.
God in His greatness will make this happen.

Many years later this special baby would indeed be born. He would be born to Joseph and Mary in a town called Bethlehem, which was known as 'the City of David'. He would be God's Chosen One. He would be a sign to the people that God loves them. His name would be Jesus.

Jesus's story is told in the New Testament.

God Calls Jeremiah

Jeremiah 1:1–9

When Jehoiakim was King of Judah, God spoke to a young man called Jeremiah. Jeremiah will now tell you his own story.

"I was very young when the Lord first spoke to me. I hadn't even grown a beard! He told me that He had chosen me to do His work. He wanted me to go and tell His people that their behaviour was wrong.

I felt very afraid; surely I was too young for such an important job. 'But Lord,' I protested, 'I don't know what to say to people!'

'Don't be afraid,' the Lord replied, 'I will give you the words and I will be with you to protect you.'

Then the Lord reached out and touched my lips. 'Here are the words you must say,' He told me. 'You must tell the people that their wicked behaviour is making me sad and very angry.'

So, knowing that the Lord God was with me, I went out to speak."

Jeremiah's Warnings

Jeremiah 1, 2

These are the words the Lord God told Jeremiah to say.

"People of Israel; you were faithful to me and I loved and protected you. But now you have turned from me: you worship idols who can do you no good. You have ruined my land, you have sinned against me. Why will you not turn back to me?"

Jeremiah soon knew how God felt. The people laughed at him and refused to listen. God told Jeremiah to warn the people.

"I will shake the land, all the birds will fly away and the fertile land will become desert. I will send armies against them; they will be taken away as captives," said God.

Jeremiah and the Potter

Jeremiah 18:1–10

Here, again in his own words, are more of Jeremiah's prophecies.

"The Lord sent me to the potter's house where I watched the man working with clay. The potter wasn't pleased with one of the pots he made, so he crushed the clay in his hands and started to make a new one.

'I am like a potter,' the Lord explained to me. 'My people are like clay in my hands. If I say I will punish them and destroy them, but they change their evil ways and become good, I will save them.

On the other hand, if I tell my people I will treat them well and make them strong, but they turn away from me and do bad things, I will crush them like clay and start again.'"

Bad Kings

2 Kings 24–25; 2 Chronicles 36:5–10

For many years, the people of Israel ignored all of the warnings Jeremiah gave them. Instead of turning back to God, both the people and their kings, one after another, continued in their cruel and selfish ways.

Of course, God was angry with them. Just as Jeremiah had warned, He sent powerful armies against His people. Nebuchadnezzar, the King of Babylonia, ordered his soldiers to destroy the Temple in Jerusalem, taking many people prisoner.

God didn't enjoy punishing His people. He desperately wanted to give them a chance to love Him again and avoid more suffering.

By now, Jeremiah was quite an old man. God sent him to visit the new King of Israel, who was called Zedekiah. Jeremiah pleaded with Zedekiah to lead the Israelites back to God, but he didn't listen.

Jeremiah tried to warn the king that God was still angry with His people, and that there would be more destruction if they continued in their wickedness. But Zedekiah ignored Jeremiah. Nothing changed.

Nebuchadnezzar

2 Chronicles 36:11–21; Daniel 1

Nebuchadnezzar's Babylonian army marched again on Jerusalem, setting up camp around the city's walls. They would not let people in or out, and they would not let food supplies into the city. Soon, the people of Jerusalem began to starve. One night, Zedekiah and many of his soldiers managed to escape, but Nebuchadnezzar hunted them down, killing some and taking others as prisoners, including the king.

The Babylonian army entered Jerusalem, where they burned down the Temple, the royal palace and many homes. They took all the healthy or skilful people back to serve them in Babylon.

Jeremiah's Letter

Jeremiah 29

Jerusalem had suffered so much destruction, there was nothing left. Many of the people remaining there fled to Egypt.

Jeremiah had told the Israelites that this would happen. He had warned them. "Why didn't they listen to me?" asked Jeremiah. "Why didn't they return to their God?"

Jeremiah's heart ached for Zedekiah, the King of Israel, and his people, so he wrote them this letter.

Work hard and pray for those who imprison you. Marry and have children so that you increase in number.

In 70 years, you will search for me with all your heart. I will answer your prayers. I will return you to your land and give you all that you hope for.

Your people who were left behind in Jerusalem will suffer war, starvation and disease. People around the world will be horrified by what happens to them.

I the Lord have spoken.

Zedekiah tore up the letter and threw it into a fire. Jeremiah wept for him.

Daniel and the King's Food

Daniel 1

When Nebuchadnezzar conquered Jerusalem, he instructed his chief servant to pick out the finest young men of the land to be trained as advisers. Daniel, along with his three best friends Shadrach, Meshach and Abednego, was among those chosen.

They were looked after well and given the same food as Nebuchadnezzar himself – but Daniel felt uncomfortable about this special treatment. He wanted to stay loyal to God and live more simply, so he refused to eat the king's food.

The chief officer was worried. "If you become too thin, the king will be furious," he said.

"Give me and my friends vegetables and water for ten days," Daniel suggested. "Then you can compare how we look with the others."

Reluctantly, the chief adviser agreed. But when the ten days were up, Daniel and his friends looked healthier than all the other young men – so the adviser agreed that they could continue their special diet.

At the end of training, all the young men were brought before the king.

"These four are the most impressive by far," he said, pointing to Daniel and his friends. "Let them become my personal servants."

Nebuchadnezzar's Dream

Daniel 2

One night, King Nebuchadnezzar had a troubling dream.

"Tell me what it was about," he ordered his advisers. "Then explain what it means."

Of course, none of them knew where to start. The king was furious. "All my advisers are fakes!" he cried. "Execute them!"

When Daniel heard what had happened, he prayed to God to help him understand the dream. Then he went before the king.

"You dreamed of a statue with a golden head," he said. "Its chest was made of silver, its thighs of bronze, its legs of iron and its feet of clay. A rock smashed the statue into tiny pieces, then the rock turned into a huge mountain that filled the Earth."

"But what does it mean?" demanded the king.

"Your empire is the head," said Daniel. "The body is made up of all the other kingdoms – none of which are as great as yours. But God will destroy them all, and build an empire that will last forever."

The Golden Statue and the Fiery Furnace

Daniel 3

Nebuchadnezzar was so impressed with Daniel that he gave him an important job in his court. Daniel made sure that his friends Shadrach, Meshach and Abednego got jobs too. They were sent to work for the king in Babylon.

"My empire is greater than all the others," boasted Nebuchadnezzar. And he decided to build a huge golden statue of himself in Babylon to remind everyone of the fact.

When the statue was finished, he ordered all the people to bow down and worship it. Everyone, from the most important ruler to the most humble peasant, obeyed. Everyone, that is, except for Shadrach, Meshach and Abednego.

"We won't bow down to a statue," they declared. "We worship only God."

When the king heard of this he flew into a rage. He sent for the three men.

"I will have you thrown in a fiery furnace," he threatened.

“God will protect us,” replied the men calmly.

So Nebuchadnezzar ordered them to be thrown into the furnace. The fire was so fierce that even the guards who threw them in were badly burned by the leaping flames. But finally the fiery furnace died down a little.

“Are they dead yet?” asked the king. What a surprise greeted his eyes! Instead of being burned to death, the three friends were alive and walking around in the flames. And not only that – instead of three, Nebuchadnezzar saw four people in the fire.

The fourth person looked like an angel of God!

Amazed, Nebuchadnezzar called to the men to climb out of the furnace. When they were examined, not a hair on their heads was harmed.

“Your God is indeed great and powerful,” he told them. Then he turned to his officials. “No one in my empire must ever speak out against their God again,” he ordered. “No other god could do such an incredible thing.”

Nebuchadnezzar's Second Dream

Daniel 4:4–18

For a while, everything went well for Nebuchadnezzar – until he had another dream, that is. Immediately, he called for his advisers, but none of them could explain what it meant. So the King summoned Daniel.

"I had a dream that made me afraid as I lay in my bed," he told him. "A tree grew until it reached the sky. It grew fruit for all to share, and animals and birds sheltered in and under it. Suddenly, an angel came down and felled it, so that only the stump was left – and then that stump turned into a man. The angel said the man must live like a wild animal, and that everyone must learn that God rules in the world."

Daniel Interprets the Dream

Daniel 4:19–27

When Daniel heard King Nebuchadnezzar's dream, he was very upset. He knew at once that it was not good news.

"I am sorry I must tell you this," he told the king. "If only this dream was meant for your enemies and not for you."

"Do not worry," replied Nebuchadnezzar. "Tell me what it means."

So Daniel explained.

"You are that tree," he began. "You provide food for your people and give them protection. But you must recognize God's power, or you will be cut down and lose your great position. You will become like the wild man, and live like an animal, eating grass. You must turn to God," Daniel warned. "Treat the poor people kindly and try to do what is right. Then these things need never happen."

The Dream Comes True

Daniel 4:28–37

One day, Nebuchadnezzar was looking down from the palace roof at the city of Babylon, when he was filled with sinful pride.

"My empire is the greatest ever," he congratulated himself. "Truly, I am the most powerful ruler in the world!"

No sooner had he spoken, than he was seized by madness, and he forgot who he was. He left his palace and, like the wild man in his dream, he roamed the countryside, living like an animal. His hair grew long and he ate grass.

For many years, this madness continued, until finally Nebuchadnezzar's mind cleared.

When he realized what had happened, he felt very foolish.

"I am not the most powerful ruler in the world," he thought. "That title belongs to God."

Nebuchadnezzar returned to his throne and ruled wisely until the end of his days.

After his death, his son Belshazzar became king, but he did not honour God.

The Writing on the Wall

Daniel 5

One night, Belshazzar held a party for his friends. All at once, a mysterious hand appeared and began to write on the wall. It wrote *Mene, Mene, Tekel, Parsin*. Belshazzar was terrified. He called for Daniel. "What does it mean?" he asked.

Daniel spoke quietly but clearly. "'Mene' means 'number'," he began. "Your days are numbered. 'Tekel' means 'weight'. You have been weighed in God's scales of justice, and have been found wanting. 'Parsin' means 'division'. Your empire will be divided up between the Persians and the Medes."

That same night, King Belshazzar's enemies burst into the palace and killed him.

Daniel in the Lions' Den

Daniel 6

After Belshazzar had been killed, Darius, the Persian leader, became King of Babylon. He chose Daniel to be one of his chief advisers, and Daniel served him faithfully for many years. Darius's old advisors soon became jealous.

"Who is this upstart?" they moaned. "Let's get rid of him."

The advisers decided to hatch a plot. They knew that Daniel prayed to God every day, so they persuaded the king to make a new law. For 30 days, no one must ask for anything from any god or human being – except from the king himself. Anyone who broke the law would be thrown to the lions!

When Daniel heard about the law he suspected that the advisors were plotting against him, but nothing would stop him from praying to God. He just carried on as he always did.

Of course, as soon as his enemies spotted Daniel praying, they rushed off to tell the king. "Daniel has broken the law!" they cried. "He must be punished!"

Darius was horrified. He realized that Daniel had been tricked – but he could not be seen to have favourites.

"I'm sorry!" he told Daniel. "You must be punished. You will be thrown to the lions. I hope your God will protect you!"

All night long, Darius tossed and turned, worrying about Daniel. At dawn, he leaped out of bed and rushed to the den.

"Has your God saved you?" he shouted.

"Yes, your Majesty!" came the reply. "God kept me safe. He knew I was innocent."

Immediately, Darius set Daniel free and arrested the men who had plotted against him.

"I shall make a new law," he declared. "Everyone must fear and respect Daniel's God. He is the one true, living God."

Cyrus's Announcement

2 Chronicles 36:22–23; Ezra 1:1–4

Before long, the city of Babylon was conquered again, this time by the Persians. So the next king of Babylon was a Persian warrior called Cyrus.

God softened the heart of King Cyrus, and made him look kindly on the people of Israel. Cyrus wrote an announcement, an important letter, to be read aloud throughout the whole of his kingdom. This is what the king's announcement said:

The Lord God of Heaven has made me ruler of all the kingdoms on earth. And He has given me the task of building a temple for Him at Jerusalem in Judah. Any of His people who are living in Babylon may go back to Jerusalem. They are to be given silver and gold, cows and sheep, and offerings for the Temple of God.

At long last, their exile was at an end. The people of Israel were to go home.

The Return to Jerusalem

Ezra 1:5–2:1; Ezekiel 45–48

The Israelites had been in Babylon for a long time. Some of them had been there for nearly 60 years and there were plenty of younger people who had never seen their homeland. But they had always dreamed of returning to Israel, and had sung songs about it, for many years.

When, at last, the Israelites were able to start the journey back home, the prophet Ezekiel took care to remind them of how they should behave. He was concerned that they should treat each other well and worship God in the proper way.

Many people travelled to Jerusalem. They were very happy to be coming home. And just as Cyrus's announcement had said, people came forward to help the Israelites. They offered them gifts of silver and gold and other valuables to be used in God's Temple when it was built.

Rebuilding the Temple

Ezra 3

When the Israelites arrived back in Jerusalem, they built an altar. It was built in the place where Nebuchadnezzar's army had destroyed the Temple built by Solomon.

Then the people hired stonemasons and carpenters. With all the gifts they had been given, they were able to buy the finest cedar wood from the neighbouring countries of Tyre and Sidon. King Cyrus had given them permission to use the most beautiful wood and to bring it into Jerusalem.

The building of God's Temple was started in springtime, two

years after the return to Jerusalem. Everyone who had been allowed to come back from Babylon joined in and set to work.

When the foundations of the Temple were finished, the priests put on their robes. They all made joyful music with trumpets and cymbals. Just as King David had done before them, they sang hymns of praise and thanks to God.

The people sang:

The Lord our God is good!
His faithful love for Israel continues for all time!

Then all the people gave a great shout of praise to God, because the foundations of the Temple had been laid.

The Temple is Finished and Dedicated

Ezra 6:15–18

Building the Temple took a long time. But it was finally finished, and very beautiful it was too.

A great celebration was arranged so that the Temple could become a holy place to worship God. This was a very joyful occasion for the people of Israel who had come home to Jerusalem after all those years in Babylon.

During the dedication ceremony, a great many animals were offered to God. Then the priests and the other people who worked in the Temple were divided into teams so that they could look after the Temple and serve God properly in the way that Moses had first described.

How happy the people were, now that they were back in their own homeland, and had a wonderful house of God right at the centre of their city.

Celebrating Passover

Ezra 6:19–22

The very next month, it was time for the Israelite people to celebrate the festival of Passover.

The priests and other temple servants prepared themselves properly. They washed in a special way, gave thanks to God, and said the right prayers for the occasion.

Afterwards, they killed the special Passover lamb for all those who had returned from exile, and for themselves to eat.

The people of Israel who had returned from Babylon were joined on this special occasion by many of their neighbours. Some of them had forgotten their true religion and had started worshipping other gods, but they realized they had been wrong. Now they wanted to worship the one true God.

There was great joy throughout the land.

Xerxes Wants a Queen

Esther 1:1–2:4

Back in Babylon, Xerxes the new King of Persia was angry with his queen, Vashti. She had made him look silly in front of his friends, so he decided to send her away and get a new queen.

The king hired people to find the most beautiful women in the country and bring them to his palace. Before they met the king, the women stayed in a separate part of the palace for a year, where they were looked after and given expensive beauty treatments. They were massaged with oil of myrrh and sweet-smelling perfumes and ointments so that they were looking their very best for the king.

The king sent for the women one at a time. After each woman had spent some time with the king, she was sent back to the join the other women. She would not return to the king unless he asked to see her again.

Esther is Chosen to be Queen

Esther 2:5–11, 17

A beautiful young girl called Esther was among the women chosen for the king. Her parents were both dead, but she had been adopted by a kind older cousin who regarded her as his daughter. This adopted father was called Mordecai, and he was a Hebrew man of the Israelite tribe of Benjamin. His family had been among those who had been exiled to Babylon by King Nebuchadnezzar.

Esther didn't tell anyone that she was Jewish, because Mordecai had forbidden it. He cared about her very much and thought it would be safer if no one knew about her family background. He came to visit her every day at the palace to check how she was.

Esther was liked by everyone who cared for her at the palace and she was given special treatment.

When her turn came to be taken before the king he thought she was the most beautiful woman he had ever seen. He soon fell in love with her and made her his queen.

Esther's Banquet

Esther 2:19–22

To celebrate Esther becoming his new queen, the king gave a grand feast in her honour. He invited all his noblemen and chief officers. As well as a magnificent banquet, he gave them all wonderful gifts and insisted that the day should be a public holiday for everyone all over the nation.

Soon after this, Esther's adopted father, Mordecai, overheard two of the guards plotting to kill King Xerxes. He went straight to Queen Esther to warn her. She passed the information on to the king. The king had the report investigated and it was found to be true. The guards were quickly arrested. Esther made sure King Xerxes knew that it was Mordecai who had saved him.

After this, the king loved Esther more than ever.

Haman's Plans

Esther 3; 5:14

A proud nobleman called Haman worked for the king. He wanted everyone to bow to him, but Mordecai refused.

"Why won't you kneel down?" people asked.

"I am a Hebrew, a Jew," said Mordecai. "I only kneel before God."

Haman was furious. He wanted to kill Mordecai and all the other Jews. So he told the king that the Jews were dangerous.

"They don't obey your laws," he said. "It shouldn't be allowed. If it pleases you, I could have them all killed."

"Do what you like with them," said the king.

He gave Haman a ring. Haman could use it to sign letters in the name of the king.

Haman sent orders to all the king's governors that the Jewish people were to be killed on the thirteenth day of the month.

Haman was pleased with the plan. He had a gallows built to hang Mordecai and the Jews.

Mordecai Asks for Help

Esther 4; 5:1–8

When Mordecai found out what Haman had done, he was very frightened and upset. He knew that Haman was one of the king's most trusted noblemen. Xerxes listened to all his advice.

Mordecai sent a message to Esther. He wanted her to go to the king and ask him to save her people. But no one was allowed to visit the king without being invited. The punishment for disobeying was death.

At first Esther was afraid of breaking the law. But Mordecai sent her another message.

"Perhaps God made you queen so that you could save your people," he said.

"I will go to the king, even though it's against the law," she said. "If I die, so be it."

Esther put on her royal gown and went to see the king. Thankfully he was pleased to see her, and forgave her for breaking the law.

"What is your request, Esther?" he asked.

"Please, will you and Haman come to a dinner I have made?" Esther asked.

The king agreed at once and sent for Haman.

Esther gave her guests a wonderful evening. She asked them to come to dinner again the next evening. So the king and Haman came again, and once more it went very well.

The King Helps the Jewish People

Esther 7:1–4

The king wanted to reward Esther. "My queen, what can I give you?" he asked. "Ask for anything and I will say yes."

Esther gathered her courage. This was the moment for her to keep her promise to Mordecai. After his feast, the king was feeling very happy. She hoped he would grant her request.

"Please, spare the lives of my people," asked Esther.

"What do you mean?" cried the king.

"My people are going to be killed," said Esther. "We are in great danger from a cruel enemy."

The king could not believe his ears. "Who has dared to do this?" he asked.

"Haman," Esther replied. When she explained, Haman was terrified. The king flew into a rage and sentenced him to death.

The law was changed to keep the Jewish people safe.

Mordecai was very pleased, and proud that Esther had been so brave.

The Jewish People are Victorious

Esther 8:8–9:32

King Xerxes gave Haman's land and houses to Esther. Then he called Mordecai to the palace and gave him Haman's job.

Mordecai became the second most important man in the kingdom. He worked hard to make sure that the people were happy and safe. The king honoured him very much, and all the Jews loved him too.

The Jewish people celebrated and feasted in every city, and every year Esther's courage in saving the lives of all her people is celebrated at the Jewish festival of Purim.

Ezra at Jerusalem

Ezra 7

Although many Jewish people had returned to Jerusalem, some had stayed behind in Babylon. One of these, Ezra the priest, wanted to go home too. So he asked permission from King Artaxerxes of Persia to go back and join his people.

King Artaxerxes gave Ezra his blessing and lots of gifts for the Temple. But when Ezra arrived in Jerusalem, he was shocked by what he saw. The people were quarrelling among themselves and disobeying God's laws. Even worse, they were worshipping statues of false gods.

Nehemiah is Sad

Nehemiah 1:1–2:3

King Artaxerxes had a servant called Nehemiah whose job was to bring him his wine. Nehemiah was a Jewish man, and many of his relations had gone back to Jerusalem.

One day Nehemiah heard some worrying news. Some men from Judea came to the court of Artaxerxes, and Nehemiah asked after the Jews in Jerusalem.

"Things are very bad in Jerusalem," said the men. "The people have forgotten God, the walls of Jerusalem have fallen down and the city gates have been destroyed by fire."

Nehemiah was upset to hear this news. He prayed to God to have mercy on his people, to forgive their sins and to help them.

When Nehemiah went to take the king his cup of wine, he could not hide his sadness.

"What has upset you?" asked King Artaxerxes. "I can see your heart is troubled."

Nehemiah was afraid, but he told the king the truth. "The city of my ancestors has been damaged," he said, "and its gates have burnt down. I am very sad indeed."

Artaxerxes' Letters

Nehemiah 2:4–8

"I don't like to see you so unhappy," the king said. "How can I help you?"

Nehemiah said, "Your Majesty, if you are willing, I would be grateful if you would send me to Jerusalem so I can help to rebuild the city."

"How long will your journey take?" asked the king. "And when will you come back?"

After Nehemiah had answered these questions, the king agreed to let him go.

Then Nehemiah said to the king, "Your majesty, would you give me letters addressed to the governors of the countries I must travel through, so that I may be able to travel safely all the way home? And please give me a letter addressed to the manager of the king's forest, asking him to give me timber. I will use the timber to make beams for the gates of the Temple courtyard, for the city walls and for a house for myself."

King Artaxerxes gave Nehemiah all the letters he had asked for. As well as this, he sent a group of soldiers to guard Nehemiah and keep him safe on his journey.

Nehemiah Rebuilds the City Walls

Nehemiah 2:11–7:3

Once Nehemiah arrived in Jerusalem, he started planning how to repair the damage. He started by riding a donkey around the walls, in order to see exactly what needed to be done. He could see that he had a lot of work to do.

Then Nehemiah called a big meeting for all the priests and other important people in Jerusalem.

"We must repair the city walls," he told them. "Our enemies think we are weak and they can attack us. We must show them we are strong. God has allowed me to come here and given me the protection of King Artaxerxes. God will help us if we trust in Him."

The people knew that Nehemiah was right. They organized themselves into working groups. Because they had many enemies, groups took it in turns to build and to keep watch for enemy attack. But they worked hard, and prayed regularly. Bit by bit, the walls grew higher.

Ezra Reads Moses' Teachings

Nehemiah 8–9

At last, the rebuilding was finished and the people had a city to be proud of. Now it was time to dedicate the Temple again and show everyone that it was God's house. Nehemiah was now governor of the city. He asked Ezra the priest to come back to Jerusalem and explain to the people how to worship properly.

Ezra was very wise. He knew a great deal about the Bible and the laws that God had given to His people through Moses. He asked everyone to come to a big, outdoor meeting in the middle of the city.

A wooden platform was built for Ezra to stand on so everyone could see and hear him. Ezra stood on the platform and read from the Laws of Moses. Everyone listened.

After a while, the people began to realize that they had not been living according to God's laws. Many began to sob.

"We are sinners," they said. "What shall we do?"

"Don't be sad," said Ezra. "If you are truly sorry, God will forgive you."

And Nehemiah said, "Today is a holy day. Go home and celebrate. Share your food with anyone who doesn't have enough. God will give you joy and strength."

So the people began to celebrate with joy. They had heard God's words and they had understood them.

They knew they wanted to worship God properly. It was nearly time for the Festival of Booths, when the Jewish people remember the 40 years they spent in the wilderness, but the people had forgotten how to celebrate this. Ezra was happy to explain to them, and they were very glad to be able to worship God again in the best way. It was time for a new beginning.

No word from
God will ever fail.

Luke 1:35

Bible Stories

The New Testament

An Angel Comes to Zechariah

Luke 1:5–25

For the many years they had been married, Zechariah the priest and his wife Elizabeth had longed for a child. But no babies came. Now they were old enough to be grandparents.

One day, Zechariah was alone in the holiest part of the Temple when he saw an angel by the altar.

"Do not be afraid" the angel said. "Your prayers have been answered. You and Elizabeth will have a son, and you must name him John. He will be a special child and will become a great prophet. He will prepare the way for God's own King."

But Zechariah said, "This can't happen – Elizabeth and I are too old to have children."

The angel replied, "All things are possible with God. But because you have not believed my words, you will not be able to speak until what I have told you has happened."

Outside the Temple, the people wondered why Zechariah was taking so long. When he finally appeared he couldn't speak and they realized that he must have seen a vision.

God's Message for Mary

Luke 1:26–38

To the north of Israel, in Galilee, there was a small town called Nazareth. A girl named Mary lived there. She was engaged to be married to Joseph, a carpenter. One day, when Mary was alone, a bright light filled the room. She looked up, and saw an angel.

"Don't be afraid," the angel said. "Peace be with you, Mary. I have a special message for you from God who has blessed you greatly. You are going to have a special baby, God's own Son, his promised King. You will call the baby Jesus."

Mary was puzzled. "How can this be?" she asked.

The angel said to Mary, "Nothing is too hard for God if you trust Him. Remember your cousin, Elizabeth, who thought she could never have children? She is expecting a baby too."

Mary trusted God, and knew she didn't have to ask any more questions. "I am God's servant," she said. "I will do whatever He asks me to do."

Mary Visits Elizabeth

Luke 1:39–56

Soon after this, Mary went to visit her cousin Elizabeth. As soon as Elizabeth saw her, she felt her own unborn baby leaping for joy to salute his little cousin. She knew then that Mary's baby would be the Saviour God had promised to send to his people. She was happy and excited and she asked for God to bless Mary and her special baby.

Mary sang a great song of praise to God, for His blessings to her, and for sending this baby who would save the people of Israel, who would lift up the humble, would feed the poor and hungry and bring hope to people who were unloved.

She stayed with her cousin for three months until it was nearly time for Elizabeth's baby to be born. Then she went home to Nazareth and to her fiancé Joseph.

The Birth of John the Baptist

Luke 1:57–80

When Elizabeth and Zechariah's baby was born, all their friends and neighbours were delighted for them. "The Lord has blessed you with this baby," they said. But Zechariah still couldn't speak.

When the time came to name the baby, all the friends and neighbours said, "Of course you will call him Zechariah, after his father."

But Elizabeth, the baby's mother, said, "We are going to call him John."

"But John is not a name used by your family – or your husband's family," the friends and neighbours said.

Then Zechariah wrote 'His name is John' in large letters on a writing tablet and showed it to everyone present. They were all amazed. Then Zechariah's speech returned and he was able to tell everyone that his son must be called John.

Jesus is Born

Luke 2:1–7

Augustus, Emperor of Rome, wanted to know how many people were in his empire. He also wanted to know if they were all paying their taxes! He sent out an order across the Roman Empire commanding that everyone return to the town where their family came from, so that their names could be written down and counted.

Joseph's family came from Bethlehem – a town in Judea. So he and Mary, now his wife, had to go back there. It was a long and tiring journey from Nazareth, especially for Mary. Her baby was due to be born very soon. At last, after travelling for many days and nights, she and Joseph arrived in Bethlehem.

All the people who had come to have their names written

down were there. The town was noisy and overcrowded. Mary and Joseph searched for somewhere to stay the night, but all the inns were full. At last, just when they were about to give up hope of finding shelter, one innkeeper offered them a place in his stable.

The shed was dirty and smelly, and full of animals. But at least it was warm and dry, and it was a place where Mary could rest.

That night, baby Jesus was born. Mary wrapped him in strips of cloth, called swaddling clothes, like all mothers did at that time. Mary and Joseph didn't have a cradle for Jesus, so Mary gently placed him in a manger, an open box for the animals' food. Soon baby Jesus was fast asleep.

The Shepherds Visit Jesus

Luke 2:8–20

That night, as usual, the shepherds of Bethlehem were looking after their sheep out on the hills above the little town.

Suddenly, the night sky above the shepherds became a blaze of light, and the angel of the Lord appeared before them. The shepherds covered their eyes because they were so afraid. They wondered what was happening.

"Don't be frightened," said the angel. "I come with good news, which will bring great joy to the whole world. A special baby has been born in Bethlehem today. He is God's promised King – your Saviour. Go and see the baby. He is sleeping in a manger."

Just then, the sky filled with a host of angels singing,

"Glory to God in the highest. Peace to everyone on Earth."

The angels disappeared, the bright light faded and the sky became dark again. The shepherds knew they had not been dreaming and, after making sure their sheep were safe, they hurried off to Bethlehem to find the special baby, God's promised King.

The shepherds found Mary, Joseph and their baby in Bethlehem, just as the angel had said. When they saw Jesus lying in the manger, they kneeled down and worshipped him.

The shepherds told Mary and Joseph all the things the angel had said to them as they tended their flocks earlier that night. Then they went back to the fields again, praising God as they went. The night of Jesus's birth was one they would never forget.

The Wise Men Follow the Star

Matthew 2:1–8

Around the time when Jesus was born, some wise men in the East noticed a special star. They knew this was a sign that a great king had been born. They decided to follow the star, to find out where it led.

The wise men packed everything they needed for their journey. They took gifts with them for the royal baby. They travelled for many days and nights, until they arrived in Jerusalem.

There, they went straight to the palace. "Where is the baby, who is born to be King of the Jews?" they asked. "We have seen his star and we have come to worship him."

King Herod was angry. He sent for his advisers and asked them about this new king, and where he could be found.

"God's prophets have written that the new king will be born in Bethlehem in Judea," they told him.

Herod sent the wise men on to Bethlehem to find the baby. "Come back and tell me where you find him," said Herod. "I want to take him a present too."

Escape to Egypt

Matthew 2:9–23

The wise men left Jerusalem and, looking up at the night skies, they were delighted to see the beautiful star that they had seen before. They followed the star and when it stopped over one of the houses in Bethlehem, they knew they had found their king. They saw the baby Jesus with his mother Mary, and kneeled before him, giving him gifts of gold, frankincense and myrrh.

God knew that Herod meant to harm baby Jesus, so He visited the wise men in a dream. He warned them not to go back to Herod, but to go home another way.

Then God sent a messenger to warn Joseph too.

"Herod wants to kill the baby," said the messenger. "You must take him and Mary to Egypt at once. Stay there until I tell you it is safe to return."

Joseph and Mary quickly gathered their things together and, in the middle of the night, they took Jesus and fled to Egypt. They stayed in Egypt until it was safe for them to go home to Nazareth.

The Boy Jesus Visits the Temple

Luke 2:41–52

When Jesus was 12 years old, Mary and Joseph took him to Jerusalem for the Festival of Passover. The celebrations lasted a whole week.

After the festival, everyone began the long journey home. Mary and Joseph thought Jesus was travelling somewhere else in their large family group. They didn't worry that they hadn't seen him for a while, as there were plenty of other people with them. It was only when evening came and everyone met together to eat that they realized Jesus wasn't anywhere to be seen.

Mary and Joseph looked for Jesus everywhere. They asked their family and friends if anyone had seen the boy. But no one had. Mary and Joseph lay awake all night worrying about their son and hoping he was safe.

As soon as daylight came, they knew they must go and look for him. So they left the group they were travelling with and hurried back to Jerusalem.

When they reached the city, they searched and searched for him. They were so worried! Finally, after three days, they went into the Temple. That was where they found their son. He was calmly sitting with the men who taught God's laws. Jesus was listening to everything they said and asking questions. Everyone was amazed at how much of the teaching he understood.

Mary and Joseph were very upset. "Your father and I have been searching everywhere for you," said Mary. "We have been so worried. How could you do this to us?"

Jesus was surprised that they had been worried at all. "I thought you would have known that I would be here in my Father's house," he said.

Mary and Joseph didn't understand what Jesus was saying to them. But they were so pleased that he was safe.

They set off for home once more, and Jesus stayed close to his parents all the way.

John the Baptist

Matthew 3:1–12; Mark 1:2–8; Luke 3:1–18

The years passed and Zechariah and Elizabeth, Mary's cousin, brought up their son John to be good and to follow God's laws.

When John became a man, he wanted some time alone to discover what God wanted him to do with his life. So he went to live on his own in the desert of Judea. It was a tough life, but John didn't mind. He was too busy talking with God.

"I want you to be my messenger, John," God told him. "You must preach my word to the people."

And that's exactly what John did. People travelled from far and wide to hear him talk.

"God's King is coming soon," he told them. "Say you are sorry to God for the things you have done wrong. Change your ways, then God will forgive you."

Many people were sorry for breaking God's laws, so John led them to the River Jordan and dipped their heads under the water. This was called 'baptism'. It was a sign that their sins had been washed away, and that God had forgiven them.

Jesus is Baptised by John

Matthew 3:13–17; Mark 1:9–11; Luke 3:21–22

Some of the people began to wonder if John could be God's promised King. But John told them, "I am preparing the way for someone much greater than me. He is so much greater that I am not even worthy to take off his shoes!"

One day, Jesus came to see John on the banks of the River Jordan.

"I have just arrived from Nazareth," he said. "Will you baptise me too?"

John knew at once that Jesus was God's promised King.

"You should baptise me, Lord," said John, falling to his knees.

But Jesus insisted. "It is what God wants," he said. So John baptised him in the river.

As Jesus came up out of the water, God's Spirit came down upon him as a dove. "This is my own blessed Son," said a voice from Heaven. "I am very pleased with him."

Jesus is Tempted in the Desert

Matthew 4:1–11; Luke 4:1–13

Jesus knew that God had very special plans for him, so he decided to go off into the desert to be alone. He wanted to pray to God and think about what he had to do.

Jesus was so busy praying and thinking that he lost track of time. Soon he had been in the desert for 40 days without eating a single meal. He was hungry and tired – and that was when Satan saw his chance to cause trouble between God and Jesus.

"If you are the Son of God, you can do anything you like," he told Jesus. "Why don't you turn those stones into bread?"

But Jesus was ready for Satan. "The Scriptures tell us that we don't just need bread to feed us," he replied. "God's words are the most important food of all."

Satan tried again. He took Jesus to the holy city and put him down on the top of the Temple roof. "If you are really God's Son," he said, "throw yourself off this roof. God will surely send his angels to save you."

These words made Jesus cross. "The Scriptures tell us that it is wrong to set tests for God," he said.

But Satan would not give up. He took Jesus to the top of a very high mountain. From here, Jesus could see many wonderful, distant lands.

"I will give you all that you can see – if you bow down and worship me," Satan tempted.

Now Jesus became really angry. "Get away from me, Satan," he shouted. "I worship and serve only God."

At last, Satan knew he was beaten and went away. Then God sent angels with food and drink to ease Jesus's hunger and thirst.

Jesus Calls the First Disciples

Luke 5:1–11; 27–31; John 1:34–51

One morning, Jesus was preaching on the shores of Lake Galilee. As the day went on, more and more people came to listen and the crowd got bigger and bigger. Everyone wanted to hear what Jesus had to say. Little by little, the crowds pushed forward, trying to get closer – until Jesus was almost standing in the water.

Just then, Jesus noticed some fishermen pulling their fishing boats up onto the beach nearby.

"Will you take me out onto the lake?" he called to one of them. The man, named Simon, was happy to help. So Jesus climbed into his boat and they rowed a little way out. Soon, Jesus was preaching to the crowds from the water.

When he had finished teaching, Jesus told Simon to take his boat further out in the lake and to drop his fishing nets into the water.

"We didn't catch any fish all night," said Simon. "But we will do as you ask."

Simon and his brother Andrew rowed the boat out into the middle of the lake. Then they dropped their nets into the water. Instantly, the nets were teeming with wriggling fish. There were so many, Simon thought the boat might even sink.

"James! John!" he called to his friends in a boat nearby. "Come and help us!"

The four fishermen were amazed. They knew that they had witnessed something very special.

"Do not be afraid," said Jesus, when the boats were safely back on the shore. "Come and follow me! From now on, you will catch people, not fish."

Over the months, Jesus called other people to follow him too. Altogether, he chose 12 men to be his closest companions and share his work. They were called his disciples.

The Wedding in Cana

John 2:1–10

One day, Jesus, his mother Mary and his disciples were invited to a big wedding in Cana. Everyone was having a wonderful time, feasting and laughing. Then, halfway through the celebrations, the wine ran out.

"Whatever shall I do?" worried the host. "The party will be spoiled for everyone."

Mary, who was helping at the wedding, called Jesus over.

“Please do something!” she whispered. “If the party is spoiled, the bride and groom will be so upset.”

“It is not the right time for me yet… ” Jesus replied.

But Mary was sure that Jesus would help. “You must do whatever my son asks you to,” she told the servants.

And Jesus did help. Nearby, there were six large empty water jars.

“Fill these with water,” he said quietly. “Then pour some out and take it to the man in charge of the party.”

The servants did as they were told. They filled up the jars, then poured out a little and handed it to the man in charge.

“Delicious,” said the man, smacking his lips – for the water had turned into the finest red wine. “Fill up the guests’ cups,” he cried. “We have kept the best until last!”

Only Jesus and the servants knew what had really happened – it was a miracle!

Jesus and Nicodemus

John 3:1–8

Nicodemus was an important Temple official. When he became interested in Jesus's teaching, he was worried that others would disapprove.

"I need to talk to Jesus without anyone knowing," he decided. Then he had an idea. "I will visit him at night, when it's dark. That way, no one will see me." And that's exactly what Nicodemus did.

"I want to learn more," he told Jesus, when they finally met. "I can see that you come from God. How else could you do the wonderful things you do?"

"If you truly want to learn more about the Kingdom of God, you must be born again," Jesus replied.

"How can I be born again?" asked Nicodemus, confused. "I'm an old man!"

"I don't mean you must become a baby again," explained Jesus. "To enter God's Kingdom, your spirit must be born again. God is not interested in how important, clever or grand you are. He wants you to have a heart that is open to Him, just like a child."

Jesus had certainly given Nicodemus a lot to think about!

The Samaritan Woman

John 4:1–26

One hot day, Jesus was travelling through Samaria. He was resting by a well when a Samaritan woman came to fetch water. "Will you give me a drink?" he asked.

The woman looked surprised. Most Jewish people looked down on Samaritans because they had different religious traditions.

"Why are you asking me?" she said. "Don't you know I'm a Samaritan?"

"If you knew who I am, you would ask me for water," replied Jesus. "I can give you the water of eternal life. If you drink it, you will never be thirsty again."

"That sounds wonderful!" replied the woman.

"Fetch your husband so that he can have some too," said Jesus.

"I have no husband," said the woman. But Jesus already knew – he knew everything about her, even though they had just met.

The woman was amazed. "How do you know so much about me?" she cried. "You must be the Messiah!" And off she ran to tell all her Samaritan friends.

The Paralysed Man and His Friends

Mark 2:1–12; Luke 5:17–26

One day, Jesus was teaching at a house in the town of Capernaum. Word spread that Jesus was in town and soon there was a crowd of people swarming outside, hoping to catch sight of him. Nobody took any notice when four men arrived, carrying their friend on a mat.

"Make way," cried the men, trying to push their way through the crowds. "Our friend cannot walk. We must see Jesus." But it was no good. There were too many people and too much noise.

"We can't give up," said one of the men. So they came up with a plan. They carried their friend up onto the mud roof of the house and dug through the surface to make a hole.

Then, they lowered him down through the opening to where Jesus was teaching, much to the surprise of everyone inside!

When Jesus saw what the men had done for their friend, he was moved by their faith. "Your sins are forgiven," he said, and turned to help the paralysed man.

There were some religious leaders among the crowd that day – and when they overheard Jesus's words they were very angry.

"Only God can forgive sin," they said to one another. "How dare he say such things!"

Jesus knew exactly what the teachers were thinking.

"Why do you feel this way?" he asked. "It's easy to say to this man, 'Your sins are forgiven,' but it's much harder to say, 'Get up and walk again.' God has given me the power to do both these things. I want you to understand that."

Then Jesus turned once more to the man on the mat. "Pick up your mat and walk!" he said.

And the man stood up and walked off in full view of everyone. "Praise be to God!" he cried.

The people were amazed. "We have never seen anything like this!" It was another miracle.

True Happiness

Matthew 5:1–12

One day, as crowds of people sat on the hillside above Galilee, Jesus told them about God's blessings. He told them that people who realized how precious God's Kingdom is would be happy.

"God will comfort those whose loved ones have died and will reward humble people," Jesus said. "Truly happy people are those who want to please God and do as he asks. If you are kind, you will receive kindness. The pure in heart shall see God. Those who work for peace will be called God's children. If people are unkind to you for doing what God asks, be happy, because God has a reward for you in Heaven."

Love Each Other

Matthew 5:13–48

To help his followers understand his teachings more easily, Jesus used everyday examples that they would understand.

"You, my followers, are like the salt we put on our food to preserve it," he said. "You will keep God's world from going bad. And the kind deeds you do will be like bright lamps shining in the darkness, giving light to the world. When people see your good work they will praise God."

Jesus also reminded the people they should follow God's laws. He told them that it was not only wrong to murder someone, it was wrong to feel angry enough to want to murder someone.

"God wants us to love our enemies," said Jesus. "He wants us to show kindness to those who do us wrong."

Teaching About Prayer

Matthew 6:5–15

Jesus also taught the people how to pray. He told them to go to a quiet place where they could think carefully about what they were saying.

Jesus said, "This is what you should say to God."

Our Father in Heaven,
May Your Holy Name be honoured;
May Your Kingdom come;
May Your will be done on Earth,
as it is in Heaven.
Give us today the food we need.
Forgive us the wrongs we have done,
As we forgive the wrongs that others have done to us.
Do not bring us to the point of temptation,
But keep us safe from evil.
Amen.

Don't Worry

Matthew 6:25–34; Luke 12:22–31

Then Jesus said, "Trust in God and He will never let you down. Don't store up riches on Earth that could be taken from you. Store riches in Heaven, where God will give you all you need. Don't worry about your next meal. God looks after the birds in the sky, and you are more important than them.

"Don't worry about your clothes. God has clothed the flowers of the fields, and he will clothe you too."

The Wise Man and the Foolish Man

Matthew 7:24–27; Luke 6:46–49

One day, Jesus told a story about two men who wanted to build houses for themselves and their families.

"The wise man," said Jesus, "was careful about where he built his house. He chose to build it on good, solid rock. The rock gave the house strong foundations. Winter came, and heavy rains and

strong winds lashed the house. But the house stood firm because of its strong foundations.

"But the second man was foolish. He didn't think carefully about where he was going to build his house. He built it on sand. The house had no foundations at all. And when the rains and storms came, his house fell down!"

Then Jesus told them, "If you follow my teachings, you will be like a person building a house on good, solid foundations. Live your lives wisely and listen to my teachings and you, too, will stand firm."

Jesus Heals

John 5:1–9; Matthew 8:1–4

There was a special pool in Jerusalem, the Pool of Bethesda. From time to time, the water in this pool would start to bubble as though an angel was stirring it. When this happened, the first sick person to get into the water would be made well.

A paralysed man had been lying by the pool for many years, unable to climb into the healing pool on his own.

One day, Jesus came past and spoke to him.

"Do you want to get well?" Jesus asked the man.

"Yes, I do," the man replied. "But I have no one to help me into the water when it bubbles."

Jesus said to him, "Stand up, and walk."

The man did as he was told. Jesus had made him well.

Another day, a man with a disease called leprosy came and knelt before Jesus.

"Lord, I know you can heal me," he said.

Jesus stretched out his hand and said, "Be healed." Immediately the man was cured of his leprosy.

The Roman Officer's Servant

Matthew 8:11–17; Luke 7:1–10

Soon after this, Jesus went to a town called Capernaum where some Roman soldiers had a camp. Generally the Jewish people hated the soldiers, but there was one Roman officer who was kind to the local people.

That day, the officer was upset. His servant had become ill, and he was very worried.

When the officer heard that Jesus was in the town he begged his Jewish friends to ask Jesus to heal his servant.

The officer's friends went quickly to find Jesus. "This Roman officer is a good man. Please help him!"

Jesus set off towards the officer's house. But before he got there, a messenger came from the Roman officer. "He doesn't think he is good enough for Jesus to come to his house. He says, 'If Jesus gives the order for my servant to be healed, as I give orders to my soldiers, then I know he will get better.'"

Jesus turned and spoke to the crowd standing nearby.

"What great faith this man has, even though he is a Roman," he said. And the servant was healed.

Jesus Calms the Storm

Mark 4:35–41

Once, when Jesus had finished his teaching for that day, he turned to his followers and said, "Let us get in this boat and cross to the other side of the lake."

So he and his friends got into the boat and set off. It was a calm evening, and Jesus was tired after a long day telling people about God. Soon, the gentle lapping of the water against the side of the boat lulled Jesus into a deep sleep.

Suddenly the wind changed and the calm water was whipped up into huge waves. The little boat pitched and tossed on the lake, and water began to wash over the sides.

The storm got worse. But all the noise and commotion did not wake Jesus.

The other people in the boat were afraid. And they were puzzled that Jesus was still asleep.

"Master, wake up! We are all going to die!" the disciples shouted.

Jesus awoke, and stood up in the little boat.

"Be still!" he ordered. Immediately, the wind died down and the water became calm.

Jesus Sends Out the Twelve

Luke 9:1–6

One day, Jesus called his twelve disciples together. "The time has come for you to go and tell people about God, and to heal the sick," he said.

Jesus sent them out in twos, so each one had a companion. He told them to take nothing for the journey and no extra clothes, but to rely on God and on the kindness of the people they met.

So the disciples set out, going from village to village, healing sick people and telling everyone about the coming of God's Kingdom.

Jesus Feeds 5000 People

Matthew 14:13–21; John 6:1–14

As time passed, there were more and more people who wanted to listen to Jesus. He would often speak to the crowd for hours at a time. Because he was so interesting, no one noticed how the time was passing by.

One day, Jesus was teaching by Lake Galilee. The day wore on and, by sunset, 5000 people or more were still gathered around him. They were all very hungry! The disciples were themselves feeling tired.

"Please send the people away," they begged Jesus. "Tell them to walk to the farms and villages to find food."

But Jesus replied. "Why don't you give them food?"

The disciples were puzzled. "Where can we get enough food to feed this crowd?" they asked.

Just then, Jesus's disciple Andrew stepped forward. "This little boy is offering his food to Jesus," he said. "He has five small loaves and two fish, but that won't feed very many people!"

Jesus said, "Tell everyone to sit down." The disciples went off to do as Jesus had said. Jesus turned to the little boy. He took the loaves and fish and thanked God for them. Then he gave the food to the disciples, who broke it up and handed it out to the people. Everyone ate as much as they needed and soon felt full. When they had finished, Jesus said to the disciples, "Gather up the leftovers."

To their surprise, the disciples gathered up twelve full baskets of leftover food!

Jesus Walks on Water

Matthew 14:22–33

After this wonderful meal, Jesus told his disciples to get into their boat and go to the other side of the lake, while he said goodbye to the crowd. Then he went into the hills to pray.

Later that night, as the wind got up on the lake, the disciples in the boat saw someone walking towards them over the water.

They were terrified. "It's a ghost," they cried. But Jesus called to them: "Don't be frightened – it is me."

Peter said, "If this is really you, Lord, tell me to come to you over the water."

"Come," said Jesus.

So Peter got down out of the boat, and walked on the water towards Jesus. But when he realized he was out on the dark lake, in the wind, he became frightened and began to sink. "Save me, Lord!" he cried.

Immediately Jesus reached out his hand to Peter and caught hold of him. "How little faith you have," he said. "Why did you doubt? Let's get back to the boat."

Together, they climbed into the boat. The others were amazed. "This must be the Son of God," they said.

Jesus Heals a Blind Man

Mark 8:22–26

Jesus healed many people who were sick and disabled. One day, he visited a place called Bethsaida. Some people brought a man to Jesus and begged him to help him. The man had been blind all his life.

Jesus took the blind man by the hand and led him out of the village. When he had touched the man's eyes and put his hands on him, Jesus asked, "Do you see anything?"

The man looked up. "I can see people," he said. "They look like trees walking around."

Once again, Jesus put his hands on the man's eyes. After this, the man could see everything as clearly as if he had never been blind.

"Go back home now," Jesus told him.

Peter Says Jesus is the Messiah

Matthew 16:13–20

By now, lots of people were talking about Jesus and the wonderful things he had done to help others. They were saying all sorts of things about who Jesus was and what these wonderful things might mean.

One day, Jesus asked his disciples, "Who do people think I am?"

They thought for a bit and said, "Some people think you are John the Baptist. Other people think you are Elijah or one of the other great prophets."

"But who do *you* think I am?" Jesus asked them.

"You are God's promised King, the Messiah. You are the one we have all been waiting for," said Peter.

Jesus was pleased when he heard this reply, but he sternly told the disciples not to tell anyone else what they knew.

The Transfiguration

Matthew 17:1–8; Mark 9:2–9

Later, Jesus went with Peter, James and John up onto a steep mountain ridge. Jesus kneeled down to pray. Peter, James and John were tired, and soon fell fast asleep.

Suddenly, they were awoken by a bright light. They looked at Jesus. Although he was still Jesus, he looked different. His face and clothes were dazzling white. There were two other shining white figures with him. The disciples knew that these were Moses and the prophet Elijah. The three of them were talking together about God's plan for Jesus, and about his death.

Peter was amazed and didn't know what to say, but he wanted to say something. So he said the first thing that came into his head.

"Lord, we make three shelters – one for you, one for Moses and one for Elijah," he babbled.

Just then a cloud passed across the sky, and the disciples heard the voice of God:

"This is my own dear Son. Listen to what he has to say!"

The disciples felt afraid and hid their faces. When they looked up, Jesus was alone again telling them it was time to head back.

As they walked back down the mountain together, Jesus told them not to tell anyone what they had seen.

Jesus Tells the Disciples He Will Die

Matthew 17:22–23; 18:21–22; Mark 9:30–32; Luke 9:43–45

Jesus realized that dangerous times were coming, and he knew it was time to prepare his disciples for what lay ahead.

"Soon I must go to Jerusalem," Jesus said. "The priests and the religious leaders do not believe that I am God's Son. I will be put to death, but I shall rise and live again after three days."

The disciples were very upset. "Never, Lord!" shouted Peter. "This must not happen to you!"

But Jesus told him he must accept what would happen and trust that God was in control.

Then Jesus warned them, "If you follow me you will meet hardships. You will suffer too."

Jesus loved the disciples, but sometimes they made him sad – especially when they quarrelled.

One day, Peter asked Jesus, "Lord, how many times should I forgive my brother if he makes me angry? Should I forgive him seven times?"

"Not just seven times," said Jesus. "You should forgive seventy times seven times – so many times you lose count."

Teaching Forgiveness

Matthew 18:21–35

Then Jesus told a story about forgiveness:

"There was once a landowner who wanted to make sure his servants had all paid him what they owed him. But one man owed him 10,000 bags of gold – and he could not pay it back.

'You will have to go to prison!' the landowner said.

'Oh please, have mercy on me!' cried the servant.

The landowner was kind. He cancelled the whole of the debt.

What do you think the servant did then? He went straight to someone who owed him 100 silver coins – not very much, but more than the man could pay. He grabbed him by the neck and shouted, 'Pay me what you owe or I will have you thrown into prison!'

When the landowner heard about this, he was very angry. 'I cancelled that huge debt you owed me,' he said. 'This man's debt is much smaller. I will have you sent to prison now.'"

Jesus is the Good Shepherd

John 10:1–15

Jesus told many other stories to let the people know how much God loved them. One day, he talked to them about shepherds.

"Anyone who goes into the sheep pen by climbing over the wall instead of walking through the gate must be up to no good," he said. "Thieves and robbers climb over walls. But the shepherd who looks after the sheep will go in through the proper gate. When he calls the sheep, they know his voice. They feel safe and they follow him."

Jesus went on to tell the people, many of whom kept sheep and knew a lot about them, that the sheep will follow a shepherd they know. "He calls them by name and leads them out of the pen, he goes ahead of them and they follow," he said. Then he added, "Sheep will never follow a stranger. They will run away from someone whose voice they do not recognize."

"I am the good shepherd," Jesus said. "The good shepherd will be prepared to die for his sheep. Someone who is looking after the sheep just as a job will not love them like that. If he sees a wolf coming, he will leave the sheep and run away. Then the wolf will be able to attack the flock and harm them.

But the good shepherd, the true shepherd who knows and loves the sheep, will not leave them. I will not leave you."

The Good Samaritan

Luke 10:25–37

Jesus was very popular, and crowds of people always gathered to listen to him teach. This made some of the other religious leaders jealous. They wanted to get rid of Jesus, and tried to catch him out by asking difficult questions.

"What do I have to do to live forever?" asked one leader.

"You know God's law," smiled Jesus. "What does it tell you to do?"

"It says I must love God with all my heart and strength and mind," answered the man. "It says I must love my neighbour too. But who is my neighbour?"

"Let me tell you a story to help you understand," replied Jesus.

"One day, a Jewish man set off on a journey from Jerusalem to Jericho. On the way, some robbers jumped out and beat him. They stole his clothes and money, and left him to die.

A little while later, a priest came by. But when he saw the body covered in blood, he quickly hurried on his way."

Priests were not supposed to touch dead bodies, and he didn't want to take any chances.

"Next, a man who worked in the Temple came along. He too saw the wounded man. 'There must be robbers on this road!' he cried in alarm, and off he hurried too.

"Finally, a Samaritan came along." Now, Jewish people and Samaritans did not like each other. "But when the Samaritan saw the injured man, he hurried over to help him. He cleaned his wounds, covered him and lifted him onto his donkey. Then he took him to an inn.

The next day, when the Samaritan had to continue his journey, he went to see the innkeeper. 'Look after this man while I am away,' he told him, handing over a bag of coins. 'When I return, I will pay any extra that is owed for his care.'"

Jesus looked at the leader who had questioned him. "Which of the three people in the story was a good neighbour?"

"The Samaritan," admitted the man.

"Then go and try to be like him," said Jesus.

The Big Dinner Party

Luke 14:15–24

One day, Jesus went for dinner at the house of a very religious family. Everyone was talking about the time when God's Kingdom would arrive on Earth. They imagined it would be like a huge party for people just like them.

Jesus smiled. "Let me tell you a story I know," he said. "A rich man decided to throw a big party for his friends. When all the delicious food was ready, he sent out his servant to invite the guests. But they all started making excuses.

'Sorry!' said one. 'I've just bought a field, and I must go and see it.'

'I need to check my new cows,' said the next.

On and on went the excuses...

'I've just got married...'

'I'm too busy...'

...until at last the servant gave up and went home to tell his master.

The rich man was furious.

'Go into the town. Invite the poor, the blind and the sick,' he cried.

The servant did as he was asked, but there was still room for more guests. So the master said to him, 'Go out onto the roads and country lanes and bring in even more people. My house will be full of the poor and the outsiders – people who others think are not important. I tell you, not one of those who were invited and made an excuse will be able to taste my wonderful feast.'"

When Jesus had finished his story the guests were silent. They realized that God welcomes everyone into His Kingdom – it's not important who you are, only that you accept His invitation.

The Lost Sheep

Luke 15:1–7

When Jesus preached about God, all sorts of different people came to listen – even robbers and thieves. But many of the religious leaders were furious when they saw Jesus talking to people who broke the law.

"How can he be a man of God if he is willing to talk to people like that?" they sneered.

"Let me explain," said Jesus, when he heard them. "Imagine that you are a shepherd with 100 sheep. Now imagine that one of your sheep is missing. What would you do? Would you just go to bed and not worry? Of course not! You would go and look for that missing sheep, and search behind every rock and bush until you found it. Then you would carry it home on your shoulders and celebrate with your neighbours.

"These robbers and thieves are like that missing sheep. They have lost their way, but I am a good shepherd. I will not forget about them. I will seek them out and tell them about God's love, to bring them safely back to Him."

The Lost Coin

Luke 15:8–10

Jesus wanted the people to know just how important each and every one of them was to God.

"Listen to this story," he told them. "There was once a woman who had just ten silver coins. One day, when she was counting them, a coin fell off the table and disappeared. Determined to find it, the woman lit her lamp and swept the house, searching in all the corners. Finally, she spotted a glint of metal under a chair. She had found it! Overjoyed, the woman called to her friends.

"'I have found the coin that was lost,' she cried excitedly. 'Let's celebrate!'

"And that's just what God does when a person who has forgotten about Him turns back to Him again!" explained Jesus. "He celebrates with all the angels in Heaven!"

The Lost Son

Luke 15:11–32

Jesus knew that people disliked him spending time with sinners.

"God loves everyone," explained Jesus. "Even when they do wrong!" And he told a story to help people understand.

"Once, there was a rich, old man with two sons," Jesus began. "When he died, the two sons would share all their father's land and money, but for now, they worked hard in his fields.

One day the younger son came to speak to his father.

'I want to leave home and see the world,' he begged. 'Can I have my share of your money now?'

The son's request made the father sad, but, because he loved him, he gave the boy his share of the money and waved him goodbye.

The younger son headed for the towns. At first he had fun spending his money on parties and new friends. But soon all the money had gone.

Things went from bad to worse. A famine swept the country and the only job the son could get was looking after pigs. He was miserable and very hungry!

'What am I doing?' the son asked himself. 'Even my father's servants have plenty to eat. I shall go home and tell him how sorry I am. I don't expect Father to take me back, but he may let me work on the land for him.'

So the son packed his bags and set off for home. He was still a long way from the house when his father spotted him. The old man ran to greet the boy, throwing his arms around him in delight.

'I'm sorry, Father,' began the son sadly. 'I have sinned.' But the landowner silenced him. Instead, he called for his servants to bring new clothes for his son. Then he told them to kill the best calf for a feast.

The older son was angry and jealous when he heard what was happening. 'Why should he have special treatment?' he complained. 'I was the one who stayed and looked after you.'

'You are always with me and everything I own is yours,' replied his father. 'Your brother has been lost, but now he is found. It is right to celebrate his return.'"

Jesus Heals a Woman on the Sabbath

Luke 13:10–17

One day, Jesus was teaching in the synagogue – the place where Jewish people study their religion. He saw a woman who had been bent over by an illness for 18 years. She was in pain and could not stand up straight at all.

When Jesus saw her, he said, "You shall be healed from your illness." Then he put his hands on her, and immediately she stood up straight and thanked God.

The officials at the synagogue were very annoyed. "Who does this man think he is?" they asked.

"Today is the Sabbath day, our special day for rest. It is against the rules to work on the Sabbath."

Jesus answered, "So which of you really does no work at all on the Sabbath? Didn't you give your animals any water this morning?"

They had to admit that they had, but that was only because they were being kind and giving the animals what they needed.

Jesus continued, "So if you are kind to your animals and give them what they need, how can you say that this poor woman should not be given what she needs too? She is more precious than your animals. She has been bent over and unable to live a normal life for 18 whole years. How can it be wrong to set her free from her illness on the Sabbath?"

The officials had no answer to this, which made them cross.

The Death and Raising of Lazarus

John 11:1–44

Two sisters, Mary and Martha, and their brother Lazarus lived in Bethany near Jerusalem. They were all friends of Jesus.

One day, the sisters sent an urgent message to Jesus. It said, "Please come quickly. Lazarus is very ill."

The disciples knew that Jesus loved Lazarus and his sisters. They felt sure that, as soon as Jesus got the message, he would rush to help the family. But instead Jesus stayed where he was, teaching and healing.

Two days later, Jesus turned to his disciples and said, "Now we will go to Bethany." The disciples were worried. They didn't want Jesus to go near Jerusalem. They knew that his enemies were plotting against him there.

But Jesus was determined to go. When he and his disciples arrived at Bethany, Martha rushed out of the house to meet them. She was very upset because Lazarus had been dead and buried for four days.

"If only you had got here sooner, then I'm sure Lazarus

would not have died," she cried.

"Lazarus will live again," Jesus reassured her. "I am the Resurrection and the Life. Anyone who believes in me will never really die. Do you believe this?"

"I do, Lord," said Martha. "I believe you are the Christ, God's Son, and that you have come to give life that lasts for ever to all who believe in you."

"Take me to Lazarus's grave," said Jesus.

Mary and Martha led Jesus to the cave where the grave was. A large stone covered the entrance.

Jesus ordered the stone to be removed, then he prayed to God his Father.

Then he called out, "Lazarus! Come out!" and Lazarus, now alive, walked out of the tomb.

Plans to Kill Jesus

John 11:45–53

Many of the people who had come to Martha and Mary's house and seen what Jesus did believed in him. But some of them went to the religious leaders, and told them what Jesus had done.

Then the priests and the religious leaders had a meeting to discuss what they should do about Jesus.

"Here is this man, healing all these people and doing miracles. If we let him go on like this, everyone will believe in him. This will be dangerous now that the Romans rule over us. They have a lot of power and will punish us by taking away our Temple."

Then one of the most important priests said to the others, "We can't let this go on. It is better for one man to die for the people than for the Romans to destroy our entire nation."

From that day onwards, the priests and religious leaders became even more keen to get rid of Jesus.

They looked around for ways to do this and for people to help them. Then some of them began to see that they might get help from someone rather surprising – one of Jesus's disciples, his special group of close followers.

One of this group was a man called Judas. He had hoped that Jesus would turn out to be a great soldier and drive the Romans away, but he was disappointed. In time, Judas decided to go and see the priests and officials. They would be waiting for him.

Jesus Blesses Children

Matthew 19:13–15; Mark 10:13–16; Luke 18:15–17

Many people thought that Jesus was so wonderful that they brought their children to meet him. They wanted him to place his hands on them and pray for them.

Jesus's disciples told them off.

"Leave Jesus alone," they said. "He's been teaching all day.

He's tired, and he needs to rest."

But Jesus stopped the disciples and called the children to him.

"Let the little children come to me," he said. "Don't stop them. The Kingdom of God belongs to people like them. This is the truth: anyone who wants to enter the Kingdom of God must be like a little child."

The happy parents brought their children forward to Jesus. He welcomed them all and blessed them.

Jesus and Zacchaeus

Luke 19:1–10

On his way to Jerusalem, Jesus passed through the town of Jericho. This was a beautiful, lush place with tall trees. Zacchaeus, the chief tax collector, lived there.

Zacchaeus was not a popular man. Everyone knew that he took more tax than he should from people so that he could keep some of the money for himself.

Crowds gathered to see Jesus as he walked by. Zacchaeus was keen to see him too. But he was a short man and couldn't see over the heads of the crowd. He knew if he tried to push his way through to the front, people would just elbow him out of the way. So he decided to run ahead and climb a tree to get a better view.

A short time later, Jesus passed by. As he walked past Zacchaeus's tree, he looked up.

"Come down, Zacchaeus," he said. "Today, I would like to come and have dinner in your house."

People in the crowd were shocked and annoyed. Why did Jesus want to mix with people like Zacchaeus? Everyone knew that he was a cheat.

But Jesus went to Zacchaeus's house, and the meeting had a remarkable effect on the tax collector. "I know I have been greedy and done wrong," he said to Jesus. "But now I want to give half of all my money to the poor." He was so happy that Jesus had shown him a better way to live his life.

Then Zacchaeus spoke to the people in the town. "I am sorry that I have taken more money than I should have done, and made you pay unfair taxes," he said. "If I have taken money I shouldn't have from anyone here, I will pay them back four times the amount."

Jesus said, "I have come to look for people like Zacchaeus who have turned away from God. I have come to bring them back to God, our Father."

Mary Anoints Jesus's Feet

Matthew 26:6–13; Mark 14:3–9

Jesus was invited to dinner by a man called Simon. While he was there, a woman called Mary came up to him with a bottle of expensive ointment. She poured it onto his feet then wiped his feet with her hair. The house was filled with a wonderful scent.

Some of the disciples thought that Mary had wasted the precious ointment. "We could have sold it and given the money to the poor," said Judas angrily.

"Leave her be," said Jesus. "Mary has done a beautiful thing to me. The poor will always be with you, and you can always do kind things for them. But you will not always have me. Mary has poured this ointment on me to prepare me to be buried."

The Greatest Commandment

Matthew 22:34–40; Mark 12:28–34

One day, some religious leaders heard Jesus teaching. They decided to test him.

"Which is the most important commandment?" they asked.

"The most important commandment," said Jesus, "is to love God with all your heart, all your soul and all your mind. The second most important commandment is to love other people as much as you love yourself. There is no commandment more important than these."

One of the Pharisees was impressed. He agreed with the things that Jesus had said.

"There is only one God," he said. "These commandments are more important than old-fashioned sacrifices and ceremonies."

Jesus could see that the man was wise and truly loved God.

"You are not far from the Kingdom of God," he said.

After that, no one dared to ask Jesus any more questions.

Jesus Enters Jerusalem on a Donkey

Matthew 21:1–11; Mark 11:1–10; Luke 19:28–40; John 12:12–15

The streets of Jerusalem were full of people getting ready to celebrate the Passover festival. A little way outside the city, Jesus arrived at the Mount of Olives. He spoke to two of his disciples.

"Go to the village ahead," he said. "As you enter it, you will find a young donkey tied up. No one has ever sat on it. Bring the donkey to me. If anyone asks you what you are doing, say that I have told you to do this, and I will return the donkey soon."

The disciples walked into the village. Soon they saw the donkey tied up just as Jesus had said. As they were untying the donkey, some people spoke to them.

"What are you doing with that donkey?" they asked.

The disciples told them what Jesus had said, and the people let them take the donkey to Jesus.

When the people in Jerusalem heard that Jesus was coming to the city, they hurried to meet him. Some of them threw down their cloaks on the road in front of him. Others cut palm branches from the trees and laid them down before him.

Crowds gathered around Jesus shouting words of praise.

"Hosanna!" they shouted. "God's promised King is coming!"

"Who is this?" asked the people of the city.

"This is Jesus," answered the happy crowds. "The prophet from Nazareth."

Everyone cheered as Jesus rode into the city like a king.

Jesus Goes to the Temple

Matthew 21:12–18; Mark 11:15–18; Luke 19:45–48

When Jesus arrived in Jerusalem, he went straight to the Temple. But when he got there, he couldn't believe what was happening. People were treating the Temple like a market. They were buying and selling things there, instead of praying to God.

Jesus looked around at the people in the Temple. There were men exchanging money for special Temple coins. There were other men buying and selling doves.

Jesus was shocked and angry.

"This is God's house," he shouted. "It is supposed to be a place of prayer, but you have turned it into a den of robbers!"

He picked up the tables and benches and threw them over. The money scattered on the floor and the doves fluttered into the air.

From that moment on, he would not allow anyone to buy and sell at the Temple.

Jesus started to teach there every day. Sick people came to him to be cured. Ordinary people were amazed at the things he said and did. The religious leaders were so angry at this that they became more determined than ever to have Jesus killed.

Jesus and His Disciples Celebrate Passover

Matthew 26:17–29; Mark 14:12–26; Luke 22:7–20

Jesus wanted to eat the Passover meal with his disciples. He sent two of them to find a place where they could eat their meal.

"Follow a man who is carrying a large water jar," he told them. "Ask at the house he enters if we may meet there."

The disciples did as Jesus had told them, and that evening the group of friends all met at the house for their Passover meal.

Jesus was sad, because he knew that this would be the last meal he would share with his friends. He took the bread, thanked God for it and gave a piece to each disciple.

"This bread is like my body," he said. "I will let my body be broken for you."

Then Jesus lifted a cup of wine, thanked God for it, and passed it around so that all the disciples could share it.

"This wine is like my blood," he said. "It will be spilled for many people."

The disciples ate and drank as Jesus had asked them to do.

Jesus Washes His Disciples' Feet

John 13:2–17

Jesus knew that the disciples had been quarrelling about which of them was the most important. He didn't want them to waste time arguing with each other. During the Passover meal, he stood up and went to fetch a basin of water and a towel. Then he started to wash the feet of his disciples.

Peter felt ashamed.

"I can't let you wash my feet," he said.

But Jesus smiled at him.

"Later you will understand," he promised.

Jesus washed all his disciples' feet, and dried them with the towel. Then he explained what he had done.

"I am your teacher and Lord, and I have washed your feet," he said. "You should do the same for each other. Follow my example. You are all equally important, because you are all servants of God."

Jesus is Betrayed

Matthew 26:31–56; Mark 14:27–50; Luke 22:39–53

That evening, after the Passover meal, Jesus and his disciples walked to a peaceful garden called Gethsemane.

"Tonight, you will all abandon me," Jesus told them.

"I would never do that!" exclaimed Peter.

"I must go and pray," Jesus said. "Stay and keep watch."

Jesus walked off by himself to pray.

"Father," he said, "will you save me from this terrible death?"

Jesus looked up and saw an angel. He knew what God's answer was.

When Jesus went back to join the disciples, they were all fast asleep. He woke them up, and again asked them to keep watch.

Twice more, Jesus went to pray. Each time, when he returned, he found the disciples fast asleep.

"Couldn't you stay awake just for an hour, for me?" he asked them sadly.

Just then, Jesus saw a row of lanterns moving towards them through the darkness.

The soldiers were coming to arrest him. The religious leaders and Temple guards were at the front of the crowd, and Jesus's disciple Judas was leading them.

As they approached, Jesus stood beside his disciples.

"I'll show you which one is Jesus by kissing him," Judas told the guards.

He walked over to Jesus and kissed him on the cheek.

The guards surrounded Jesus. Angrily, Peter cut off the ear of the chief priest's servant.

"No, Peter!" ordered Jesus.

He touched the man's wounded ear and healed it.

"You have come armed with swords," Jesus said to the guards. "Do you think I am a criminal?"

The guards didn't reply. They arrested Jesus and took him out of the garden. The disciples abandoned him to the guards, just as Jesus had said.

Jesus is Crucified

Matthew 27:15–61; Mark 15:6–47; Luke 23:13–55

The chief priest said that Jesus claimed to be the Son of God, which was against the law. They wanted to kill him. But the Roman governor Pontius Pilate believed that Jesus was innocent, and wanted to release him. He took Jesus before a crowd of Jewish people.

"This man is innocent. Do you want me to kill your King?" he asked.

"Crucify him!" shouted the mob.

So Pilate sentenced Jesus to death. Jesus had to carry a huge wooden cross to a place called Golgotha. Along the way, the crowd laughed and made fun of him. At Golgotha, the soldiers nailed Jesus to the cross. They put a sign above his head saying 'Jesus, King of the Jews.'

Two robbers were nailed up on either side of Jesus. Then the soldiers settled down to wait for Jesus and the two robbers to die. Jesus felt sorry for them.

"Father, forgive them," he prayed. "They don't know what they're doing."

"If you're the Son of God, why don't you save us?" asked the first robber.

"Be quiet," said the second robber. "We are guilty, but this man is innocent. Please remember me, Jesus, when you come again as King."

"You will be with me in Paradise today," Jesus promised.

Jesus suffered terribly for hours.

"My God! Why have you left me?" he called out.

At three o'clock, he knew that he was about to die.

"It is finished," he cried.

Later that day, Jesus's friends wrapped his body in strips of linen, sprinkled with special spices. Then they placed the body in a cave tomb and used a big stone to block the entrance.

Jesus Rises from the Dead!

Matthew 28:1–10; Luke 24:1–12; John 20:1–18

Very early on the third day after the crucifixion, a friend of Jesus, called Mary Magdalene, went to visit his tomb. She was heartbroken, and wanted to take some sweet-smelling spices she had prepared for his body. But when Mary arrived, the stone blocking the entrance to the tomb had been rolled away. When she looked inside she discovered that Jesus's body was gone!

"Someone must have taken him!" she wept.

Suddenly, two men in dazzling white gowns appeared. They were angels, sent by God.

"Do not be afraid," the angels told her. "Jesus has not been taken. He has risen, just as he said he would."

At these words, Mary remembered what Jesus had once told them all – that he would be crucified and buried, but that he would rise again.

"I must tell the others!" she cried, hardly daring to believe that Jesus might be alive.

And off she ran, calling for the disciples.

At the sound of her cries, Peter and John rushed to the tomb. But all they could find were the linen cloths that Jesus had been wrapped in.

"Stay here," they told Mary. "We'll go and find the others to tell them what has happened."

As Mary waited in the garden, she suddenly sensed someone behind her.

"What's the matter?" asked a kindly voice.

"Jesus's body is gone," she whispered, staring at the ground.

"Mary!" said the stranger. "Do you not know me?"

Mary looked up and at once and her heart leapt. It was Jesus. He really was alive!

Jesus Appears to His Disciples

Luke 24:13–19; John 20:19–21:14

That same day, two of Jesus's friends were walking home. They hadn't heard Mary's wonderful news, and were feeling very sad.

"What will happen now?" they asked each other miserably. They were so busy talking that they didn't notice a stranger appear beside them.

"What's the matter?" the stranger asked them. So one of them, Cleopas, explained.

"We thought Jesus, our master, was the Messiah, but now he is dead and all our hopes are gone!"

The stranger smiled. "Remember what the Scriptures say," he told them. "The Messiah has to die – not for his crimes, but to pay for the sins of others. His death shall bring God's forgiveness for everyone."

The two friends listened to the stranger all the way home. When they reached their door, they invited him in for a meal. But it wasn't until they all sat down at the table – and the stranger thanked God for the food – that they suddenly recognized him.

"Can this be our master?" the friends gasped in astonishment… but as they moved towards him, the stranger disappeared.

The two friends danced around the table with joy. "It was Jesus," they cried. "We're sure of it! We must share the news." And off they rushed to find the disciples.

Of course, the disciples already knew that Jesus was alive. They all talked excitedly about what had happened, hardly daring to believe it – until Jesus arrived to share a meal with them, that is.

"Master!" they cried. "Is it really you?"

"Peace be with you!" said Jesus. And he showed them his wounds, so that they could be sure.

The disciples were overjoyed. "You truly are here!" they cried.

Only one disciple, Thomas, was not there to see Jesus return.

"I don't believe you!" he said flatly, when the others told him that Jesus was alive. "I need proof." And he refused to listen.

A week later, Jesus appeared to the disciples again, and this time Thomas was there.

"Touch my wounds and believe," said Jesus, holding out his hands to Thomas. "Your eyes tell you to believe, but there is a special blessing for those who can believe without seeing."

Jesus is Taken up to Heaven

Luke 24:50–53; Acts 1:6–11

There could be no doubt that Jesus really was alive. Over the next month, he appeared to the disciples many times. He knew that the time was coming when he would have to leave them for good, and he wanted to get them ready for what lay ahead. Sometimes he just chatted and shared food with them, at other times they prayed together, but most often Jesus talked about what had happened, and what it meant.

At last, the day came when Jesus knew that he must finally say goodbye to his companions. "Soon, I will return to my Father in Heaven," he told them. "You won't see me again, but I want you to carry on teaching God's word to the people, just as I did. I want you to baptise them in my name. I want you to spread God's word to the whole world."

The disciples looked troubled. "How will we manage without you?" they asked. But Jesus knew that they were ready to take on the task.

"Don't worry," he replied. "I will send my Holy Spirit to be with you."

Then Jesus held up his hands to bless them – and in that instant, he left the disciples and rose up into Heaven.

As they watched Jesus disappear into the clouds, the disciples were filled with a feeling of great joy, and they fell to their knees in worship.

"We must return to Jerusalem and pray," they told each other. "We must wait for the gift of the Holy Spirit to come to us."

The Gift of the Holy Spirit

Acts 2:1–8

The disciples knew that the Holy Spirit would bring them close to Jesus in a new and different way, but they had no idea how or when this wonderful gift would come. So they decided to return to Jerusalem and pray for guidance.

At last, on the Jewish Festival of Pentecost, their prayers were answered. A great rush of wind came from Heaven, filling the house where they were staying.

A feeling of great warmth filled them, so that their hearts were bursting with happiness. It was just as if Jesus was with them, right there in that house.

The disciples went out into the streets, pouring out their joy in words of praise, thanking God for this wonderful gift. Even more amazing, everyone who heard them could understand their words – no matter what language they spoke. It truly was a gift from God!

The Early Church

Acts 2:43–47

Many people who met the disciples, and heard them speak, were deeply moved. The disciples themselves were able to heal people and work miracles, just as Jesus had done.

All the people who believed in Jesus lived happily together, and shared everything they owned. They sold what they had and divided the money among the other believers, making sure that everyone had what they needed. Every day they all went to the Temple to worship together. Then they met in each other's homes, to pray together and to share meals joyfully.

They were always happy and praising God. Other people noticed the way they lived and how happy they were, and wanted to find out more.

So every day, more and more people turned to God and started to find out about Jesus. They came to love God and follow his laws.

The Beautiful Gate

Acts 3:1–10

One afternoon, Peter and John were on their way to the Temple to pray. A man who had been lame from birth and who could not walk was sitting by the Temple gate, known as the Beautiful Gate. This is where he sat every day, to beg from the people as they went in.

When the man saw Peter and John coming up to the gate, he asked them to give him something.

Peter and John looked at the man, and then Peter spoke.

"If you are hoping we will give you silver or gold, I am afraid we have none to give you," he said. "But I will certainly give you what I do have."

Then he said, "In the name of Jesus, get up and walk!"

Peter took the man by the hand and helped him up. At once the man's feet and legs became strong, and he sprang up, stood and then walked. Then he went into the Temple with them, where he walked about and jumped up and down. And he praised and thanked God at the top of his voice.

Everyone recognized the man as the beggar who used to sit at the Beautiful Gate. They were all amazed.

Saul is Converted and Starts to Tell About Jesus

Acts 9:1–30

There was a man called Saul, who was very angry at the disciples and other believers. He thought that they were threatening the true religion. He wanted all the followers of Jesus to be put into prison or killed.

Saul asked the religious leaders to let him go to Damascus in Syria, to bring back any new Christians and punish them. But on the way, something amazing happened to him. Suddenly, a great light from Heaven shone down on him. He fell to the ground. Then he heard a voice saying, "Saul! Saul! Why are you hurting me?"

"Who are you?" Saul asked.

The voice replied, “I am Jesus, and you are attacking my followers! Now get up and go into the city, and you will be told what to do.”

Saul picked himself up and opened his eyes, but he couldn’t see anything at all. The people travelling with him led him into Damascus. But he was blind for three days, until God sent a man called Ananias to go and see him and restore his sight.

Ananias was frightened at first, because he had heard all about Saul and how he wanted to kill all Christians. But he obeyed God.

Saul was baptised and changed his name to Paul. He started telling everyone how wonderful Jesus was. “He is indeed the Son of God!” he said. Everyone who heard him was amazed.

The Christians in Damascus were delighted that Saul, now called Paul, believed in Jesus, but not everyone was glad. The people who had wanted him to continue in his old ways were so angry that they tried to find a way of killing him. Fortunately Paul found out about this and, during the night, some of the other believers helped him to escape from the city by hiding him in a large basket and lowering him down through a window in the city wall.

Peter Has a Dream

Acts 10:9–16

One day, while Peter was staying at a house in Joppa near the sea, he went up on the roof to pray. It was nearly time for dinner and he was hungry. But then he dozed off and began to dream.

He saw the sky open and a large sheet coming down towards him. In the sheet were all sorts of animals.

A voice said: "Get up, Peter. Kill something to eat."

Peter was shocked. There were a lot of animals his people never ate because they believed that God had told them not to. All the animals in the sheet were like this.

"I can't do that," he said, "I am not allowed to eat these animals. They are unclean."

But the voice said, "God has made them clean."

This happened three times, then the animals disappeared.

Peter Understands the Dream

Acts 10:17–48

While Peter was wondering what his dream could mean, some men came looking for him. They had been sent by an important Roman general called Cornelius.

The men told him that an angel had come to Cornelius and asked him to send for Peter. Jews were not supposed to go to the houses of Romans, but Peter realized that God wanted him to go, so he agreed.

When he came to Cornelius's home, the general fell to his knees at Peter's feet. "I am eager to hear your message," said Cornelius. So, Peter told the general and his family all about Jesus. Cornelius was so moved by Peter's words that he and all his family were baptised.

Peter now understood the meaning of his dream. God does not have favourites, but is happy to welcome people from everywhere if they want to follow Him and do what is right.

Paul's Missionary Journeys

Acts 13–21

When he was known as Saul, Paul had led people to capture and arrest Christians. But he completely changed after he became a Christian himself. He wanted to spread the good news about Jesus – not just to Jews but to anyone who would listen. Paul himself was from Tarsus (in what is now Turkey). He was Jewish, but he had grown up among people who were not Jewish.

Paul and his friend Barnabas set off to preach about Jesus in other places. First they travelled to the island of Cyprus. There Paul blinded a magician named Elymas who had made fun of the Christian message. That event, early in Paul's first journey to teach God's word, showed that he was not afraid to stand up to those who were against him. It also showed that he had special strengths – and he would need those strengths to overcome many hardships to come.

Paul travelled by boat across the eastern Mediterranean to tell people about Jesus. He went through much of Greece and Macedonia. He also visited many places in what are now Turkey, Syria and Lebanon. Paul met other Jews wherever he went, and he would pray with them. But he said that Jesus's message was for everyone, not just for Jews. Many different people listened, and became believers in God.

The people that Paul met on his travels spoke different languages, dressed differently and had different religions. But their countries were all part of the Roman Empire, so the Romans could order them around. Roman citizens had more rights than non-citizens. Many of these people welcomed Paul's message that Jesus had come to save everyone – not just Jews or Romans.

Paul and Silas in Prison

Acts 16:16–34

In the city of Philippi, Paul and his friend Silas drove an evil spirit from a servant girl. Her angry masters dragged the pair in front of the Roman rulers.

"These men are Jews and are making trouble in our city," they shouted. A crowd joined in and soldiers beat Paul and Silas and threw them into jail. The jailer was told to guard them well.

About midnight, Paul and Silas began praising God. Suddenly the whole building shook, the prison doors flew open and the prisoners' chains fell open. The jailer thought everyone had escaped. He was so frightened of being blamed he decided to kill himself, but Paul called out, "Stop. We are all here."

The joyful jailer asked how he could be saved. Paul and Silas answered, "Believe in the Lord Jesus." The jailer took Paul and Silas to his home, where he and his family were baptised as believers.

Paul is Shipwrecked on Malta

Acts 27:1–28:11

Paul was making the long journey to Rome on a ship. It sailed through terrible storms and high seas. An angel told Paul that the ship and its cargo would be lost, but not the hundreds of people on board. Paul calmed the others with this message.

The ship ran aground on the island of Malta. Waves broke it up and washed the cargo away. But the people made it to the shore. There some kind islanders built a fire to warm the travellers. The flames disturbed a dangerous snake, which bit Paul's hand.

The people of Malta expected Paul to die. But he flung the snake into the fire and wasn't hurt at all. The people could see that God had protected Paul. They listened to his message and became Christians.

Paul Writes Many Letters from Prison in Rome

Acts 28:11–31

Paul spent a winter spreading the Christian message on the island of Malta. Then he boarded a ship on its way from Egypt to Rome. It stopped for three days in Sicily and then travelled up the west coast of Italy.

Christians there had learned of Paul's arrival. The kind officer Julius let Paul stay with some Christians for a week in the city of Puteoli. Other Christians travelled a long way to see him.

Paul was put in prison in Rome for telling people about God and Jesus. But he was allowed to live alone with just one guard.

He sent for Rome's Jewish leaders and told them of his mission. He explained that God kept his promise to love and care for his people by sending Jesus.

Paul also said that he had chosen to go as a prisoner to Rome because he was a Jew. He said, "I am bound with this chain because I believe in the hope of Israel."

Paul then reminded the Jewish leaders of the words the Holy Spirit had spoken to their ancestors:

"You will listen and listen, but you will not understand. You will look and look, but you will not learn."

He added that all people could share the Good News of Jesus even if many people chose not to do so: "I want you to know that God has also sent his salvation to those who are not Jewish, and they will listen!"

Paul stayed for two years in Rome. He preached to many people. He also wrote letters to many of the Christian groups he had visited on his travels. In one of those letters, to the Christians of Philippi, Paul finds hope even though he is being kept prisoner:

"Because I am in prison, most of the believers have become bolder in Christ and are not afraid to speak the Word of God."

The Church is Like a Body

1 Corinthians 12:12–27

Paul remembered all of the groups of Christians that he visited and the new churches he had helped to set up. He wrote many letters to these Christians, even when he was hundreds of miles away from them. Those letters gave hope and advice to the believers. They also helped those Christians understand that they were all part of a much larger group – the whole Church.

Paul's first letter to the Christians in Corinth explained much of what he believed. Corinth was an important and wealthy city in the Mediterranean. All sorts of people passed through its streets – rich and poor, European and Asian, Greeks, Romans,

Jews and many others. But Paul wanted to show that the Christian message was for all of those people. He wrote:

"We were baptised by the same Holy Spirit; Jews as well as Greeks, slaves as well as free men."

He continued by comparing the Church to a body. "It consists not of one member, but of many, all with different roles and talents." A body has different parts – eyes, ears and feet, for example – each doing a different job, but dependent on the others: "If one part is hurt, all the parts share its pain."

Paul made this even clearer by telling the Corinthians, "We, who believe in Jesus, are like his body here on Earth. Each of us has an important part to play in the Church."

Love is the Greatest Gift

1 Corinthians 13

Paul spelled out a simple message in a letter to the Christians of Corinth: the most important thing in life is love. The gifts that we think are important matter much less than love. We can speak many languages, predict the future or even give all our things to the poor. None of these does any good without love.

"I may have faith so great I can move mountains. But even with all these things, if I do not have love, then I am nothing."

Paul told the people how he began to see things differently as an adult from how he had seen them as a child. In the same way, we will all see things differently when we fully understand Christ's message. But, Paul said, "These three things continue for ever: faith, hope and love. And the greatest of these is love."

Teaching About the Tongue

James 3:1–12

James was another great leader of the early Church. He wrote about how easy it is to go wrong, and how often it is because of something we've said.

"We all make many mistakes. If people never said anything wrong, they would be perfect and able to control their entire selves too."

What we say, of course, depends on using our tongue. James wrote, "It is a small part of the body, but it boasts about great things." Like the rudder of a ship or the bit in a horse's mouth, the tongue can guide something much bigger. That gives the tongue great power to do good or bad. James says we can use the tongue to hurt people, but we can say sorry with it too.

John Has a Vision of Heaven

Revelation 21, 22

The Bible ends with John's wonderful vision of Heaven. This vision is called Revelation, which comes from the word 'reveal'. To reveal something is to show it clearly. John wrote down just what was revealed to him in his vision.

In his vision, John saw Jesus, and his face was shining because he was so holy. He was on his throne in Heaven, and there were angels, people and living creatures all around him, worshipping him and singing songs to him.

An angel spoke to John and explained that because people have forgotten to worship God and haven't looked after the world that he made, the world will eventually be destroyed. But God will create a new Heaven and a new Earth for his people. John describes what happened in his vision:

"The first Heaven and the first Earth had disappeared, and there was no sea any more. And I saw the holy city, the new Jerusalem, coming down out of Heaven from God."

This is a wonderful vision of eternal life for those who have pleased God.

They will live in this beautiful city. There will be no need for special temples because God will be with them always. John learns of even more wonders about God's presence among His people:

"He will wipe away every tear from their eyes, and there will be no more death, sadness or pain, because all the old ways are gone."

An angel guides John through most of his vision, explaining each wonder. But the vision ends with Jesus himself. He agrees with what the angel has said. He then promises:

"Jesus, the One who says these things are true, says 'Yes, I am coming soon.'"

Let them praise
the name of the Lord,
for his name alone is great.

From Psalm 148

Prayers

Original prayers by Meryl Doney and Jan Payne

Wonderful World

God made the world so broad and grand,
Filled with blessings from his hand.
He made the sky so high and blue,
And all the little children too.

Anonymous

For this new morning and its light,
For rest and shelter of the night,
For health and food, for love and friends,
For every gift your goodness sends,
We thank you, gracious Lord.

Anonymous

Dear God, bless our nets as we cast and trawl;
The ocean is deep and our ship is small.

Traditional

Bright is the morning,
New is the day;
When I wake,
To God I say –
"Good morning!"

Cool is the evening,
At close of day;
Before I sleep,
To God I say –
"Good night!"

Original

For flowers that bloom about our feet,
Father we thank thee.
For tender grass so fresh, so sweet,
Father we thank thee.
For the bird and hum of bee,
For all things fair we hear or see,
Father in heaven, we thank thee.

Ralph Waldo Emerson

God who made the Earth,
The air, the sky, the sea,
Who gave the light its birth,
Careth for me.

Sarah Betts Rhodes

Wide as the world,
Deep as the sea,
High as the sky,
Is your love for me.

Original

Lord, make me see your glory in every place.

Michelangelo

I may be small,
But I can sing
A song of praise
To God the king.

Original

He prayeth best, who loveth best
All things both great and small;
For the dear God who loveth us,
He made and loveth all.

Samuel Taylor Coleridge

Snowdrops,
Ice drops,
Raindrops
Fall.
Sun shines down
To kiss them all.
See them sparkle in the light,
Winter's wonders
Jewel-bright.
Snowdrops,
Ice drops,
Raindrops
All,
Show God's love
For great and small.

Original

O God! who giv'st the winter's cold,
As well as summer's joyous rays,
Us warmly in thy love enfold,
And keep us through life's wintry days.

Samuel Longfellow

Praise the Lord! Praise him on Earth, praise him in heaven.
Praise him for the wonderful things he has done,
and just for being God.

From Psalm 150

We can praise God on the trumpet,
We can praise him on the drum,
We can praise him with our dancing,
We can whistle, shout or hum.
We can praise God on the violin
Or use our voice to sing,
We can make a very joyful noise
On almost anything!

Original

Two eyes to see, two ears to hear,
one nose to smell, one mouth to tell.
How great is God who gave them to me.

Original

Dear God,
Thank you for the sun so bright
That fills the world with dazzling light.
And thank you for the muffled sound
When snow lies thickly on the ground.

A special thanks for gentle rain,
Which helps the grass grow green again.
But please, God, send the wind, I pray
So I can fly my kite today.

Original

Summer suns are glowing
Over land and sea,
Happy light is flowing
Bountiful and free.
Everything rejoices
In the mellow rays,
All Earth's thousand voices
Swell the psalm of praise.

Bishop How

God bless the field and bless the furrow,
Stream and branch and rabbit burrow.
Bless the minnow, bless the whale,
Bless the rainbow and the hail.
Bless the nest and bless the leaf,
Bless the righteous and the thief.
Bless the wing and bless the fin,
Bless the air I travel in.
Bless the mill and bless the mouse,
Bless the miller's bricken house.
Bless the earth and bless the sea,
God bless you and God bless me.

Anonymous

Thank you for the special time
When winds begin to blow
And golden leaves come tumbling down
Setting the earth aglow.

I know the summer's over now,
And winter's on its way,
But I am full of happiness
On this colourful, bright day.

Original

Giving Thanks

For health and strength and daily food,
we praise your name, O Lord.

Traditional

Be present at our table, Lord;
Be here and everywhere adored.
Thy creatures bless, and grant that we
May feast in paradise with thee.

John Wesley

Bless, dear Lord, my daily food
To make me healthy, strong and good.

Original

Just a glass of warm milk,
Just a slice of bread,
Thank you for these good things
On my way to bed.

Original

I pray that ordinary bread,
Be just as nice as cake;
I pray that I could fall asleep,
As easy as I wake.

Anonymous

Dear God,
Thank you for all the wonderful food
And letting me taste it.
Help me think of others too,
And not to waste it.

Original

Oh, the Lord is good to me,
And so I thank the Lord
For giving me the things I need,
The sun, the rain and the apple seed.
Oh, the Lord is good to me.

John Chapman, "Johnny Appleseed"

Somebody sowed it, somebody watered,
Somebody weeded and hoed,
And God gave the sun, the wind and the rain
To bring us this harvest of food.

Original

Father, we thank thee for this food,
For health and strength and all things good.
May others all these blessings share,
And hearts be grateful everywhere.

Traditional

For what we are about to receive
may the Lord make us truly thankful.

Anonymous

The bread is warm and fresh,
The water cool and clear.
Lord of all life, be with us,
Lord of all life, be near.

African grace

Thank you, God, for this day,
this family and this food.

Original

Dear God,
Help me share
All that you have given me
With your children
Everywhere.

Original

It is very nice to think
The world is full of meat and drink,
With little children saying grace
In every far-flung kind of place.

Robert Louis Stevenson

Thank you for visits
And all kinds of treats.
Thank you for walking
Down different streets.
Thank you for good times
Wherever we roam.
But most of all, God,
Thank you for home.

Original

Each time we eat, may we remember God's love.

Prayer from China

May we who have much remember those who have little.
May we who are full remember those who are hungry.
May we who are loved remember those who are lonely.
May we who are safe remember those who are in danger.
May we who have so much learn to share.

Original

Jesus, you fed many people with only
five loaves of bread and two fishes.
Help us to share what we have with others.

Original

All good gifts around us,
Are sent from heaven above,
Then thank the Lord, O thank the Lord,
For all his love.

Matthias Claudius

God is great,
God is good,
Let us thank him
For this food.

Anonymous

Family and Friendship

Peace be to this house and to all who dwell here.
Peace be to those that enter and to those that depart.

Anonymous

Jesus bless our home today,
Be known in all we do and say.
When there's trouble, be our guide,
Bless everyone who steps inside.

Original

I live for those who love me,
Whose hearts are kind and true;
For the heaven that smiles above me,
And awaits my spirit too;
For all human ties that bind me,
For the task my God assigned me,
For the bright hopes left behind me,
And the good that I can do.

George Linnaeus Banks

God bless all those that I love.
God bless all those that love me.
God bless all those that love those that I love,
And all those that love those that love me.

From an old New England sampler

May the road rise to meet you.
May the wind be always at your back.
May the sun shine warm upon your face,
the rains fall soft upon your fields,
and, until we meet again, may God
hold you in the palm of his hand.

Irish blessing

All people that on Earth do dwell,
Sing to the Lord with cheerful voice;
Him serve with mirth, his praise forth tell;
Come ye before him and rejoice.

Scottish Psalter

Sometimes I'm up, sometimes down,
My thoughts are like a seesaw.
But I thank God you're always there;
That's what friends are for.

Original

Dear God, thank you for good friends.
Thank you for the way they listen to me,
understand what I need, and try to help.
Help me be a good friend right back again,
listening to them, hearing what they say, and
always being there for them when they need me.

Original

You made the people that I meet,
The many people, great and small,
In home and school and down the street,
And you made me to love them all.

J. M. C. Crum (adapted)

Jesus, friend of little children,
Be a friend to me;
Take my hand, and ever keep me
Close to thee.
Never leave me, nor forsake me;
Ever be my friend;
For I need thee, from life's dawning
To its end.

Walter J. Mathams

Sometimes it's not easy to make friends, dear God.
Help me begin by being friendly to others.

Original

I have
quiet friends,
noisy friends,
funny ones and sad,
many friends,
few friends,
sensible and mad,
good friends,
naughty friends,
tall friends and short;
thank you, God,
for giving me
friends of every sort.

Original

Dear God, bless all the children who have
no family. Please look after them and
send them someone who will care for
them so that they will not be alone.

Original

Lord, may your angels bless
and guard all those I love.

Original

Dear God, thank you for my family and the
things we do together. Thank you for the meals
we eat, for the jokes we share, for the TV
we watch, for the place where we live. Help us
remember that we are part of your family.

Original

Dear Father, thank you for my friends.
Help me be a good friend to them.
Bless them and keep them safe,
today and always.

Original

Look after my family when we have to be apart. Thank you for the thoughts we share, the phone calls we make, the messages we send, the memories we keep, the prayers we pray. Help us remember that you are with us all.

Original

Love is giving, not taking,
Mending, not breaking,
Trusting, believing,
Never deceiving,
Patiently bearing
And faithfully sharing
Each joy, every sorrow,
Today and tomorrow.

Anonymous

May our friendship last
though we are apart.
May our friendship last
when we are busy.
May our friendship last
even when we make new ones.
May our friendship last
as long as we live.

Anonymous

Animal Blessings

Dear God, I heard
The song of a bird,
Singing for joy in the morning.
It made my heart sing
Like anything
That I am alive, like him.

Original

The song of the wren,
The smallest bird,
Is the biggest and strongest
I've ever heard.
He's praising God
For his little nest,
And I think he'll burst
With happiness!

Original

Lo, the winter is past, the rain is over
and gone, the flowers appear on the earth,
the time of the singing of the birds is come,
and the voice of the turtle dove is heard
in the land.

From The Song of Solomon

Hurt no living thing:
Ladybird, nor butterfly,
Nor moth with dusty wing,
Nor cricket chirping cheerily,
Nor grasshopper so light of leap,
Nor dancing gnat, nor beetle fat,
Nor harmless worms that creep.

Christina Rossetti

From ghoulies and ghosties,
long-leggety beasties, and things
that go bump in the night,
good Lord deliver us.

Traditional

No shop does the bird use,
No counter nor baker,
But the bush is his orchard,
The grass is his acre.
The ant is his quarry,
The seed is his bread,
And a star is his candle
To light him to bed.

Elizabeth Coatsworth

To all the humble beasts there be,
To all the birds on land and sea,
Great Spirit, sweet protection give
That free and happy they may live!

Original

Thank you for the beasts so tall,
Thank you for the creatures small.
Thank you for all things that live,
Thank you, God, for all you give.

Anonymous

Loving Shepherd of thy sheep,
Keep thy lambs, in safety keep;
Nothing can thy power withstand;
None can pluck them from thy hand.

Jane Eliza Leeson

Dear Father, hear and bless
Thy beasts and singing birds,
And guard with tenderness
Small things that have no words.

Anonymous

I come in the little things,
Saith the Lord:
Not borne on the morning's wings
Of majesty, but I have set My feet
Amidst the delicate and bladed wheat.
I come in the little things,
Saith the Lord:
Yea! On the glancing wings
Of eager birds, the softly pattering feet
Of furred and gentle beasts.
I come in the little things,
Saith the Lord.

Evelyn Underhill

The lark's on the wing;
the snail's on the thorn:
God's in his Heaven –
all's right with the world!

Robert Browning

I heard a lark singing this morning.
He flew straight up into the blue sky,
singing for all he was worth.
Help me learn how to praise you,
Lord, as gladly as that lark.

Original

Said the robin to the sparrow,
"I should really like to know
why these busy human people
seem to fret and worry so."
Said the sparrow to the robin,
"Friend, I think that it must be
that they have no heavenly Father
such as cares for you and me."

Traditional

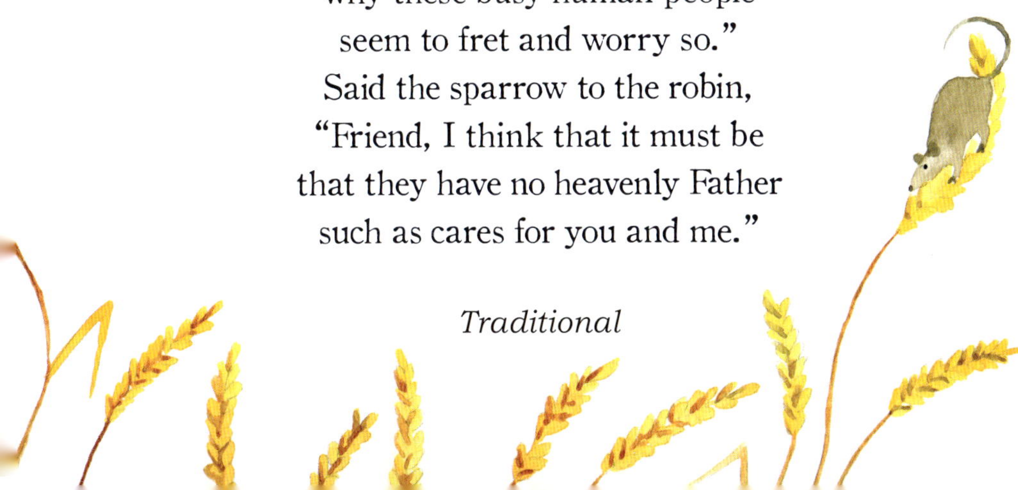

Lord, you have made so many things!
How wisely you made them all!
The Earth is filled with your creatures.

From Psalm 104

O heavenly Father, protect and bless all things that have breath:
guard them from all evil and let them sleep in peace.

Albert Schweitzer

Dear God,
our pets are very special.
They give us love and
many happy hours.
They teach us how to love
and look after them.
Thank you.

Original

Please God, you know how much we love our pet, and now our pet is not very well. Please help us look after our pet. Help the vet know how to treat this little animal and, if possible, to make our dear pet better again.

Original

God bless the animals
Great and small,
And help us learn
To love them all.

Original

Following Jesus

Father God, who gave me life,
help me live for you.

Original

Teach me, my God and king,
In all things thee to see,
That what I do in anything
To do it as for thee.

George Herbert

Teach us, Lord, to serve you as you deserve,
to give and not to count the cost, to fight and
not to heed the wounds, to toil and not to seek
for rest, to labour and not to ask for any reward
save that of knowing that we do your will.

St Ignatius Loyola

Move our hearts with the calm, smooth flow of your grace.
Let the river of your love run through our souls.
May my soul be carried by the current of your
love, toward the wide, infinite ocean of heaven.

Gilbert of Hoyland

Lord, teach me all that I should know;
In grace and wisdom I may grow;
The more I learn to do thy will,
The better may I love thee still.

Isaac Watts

What can I give him,
Poor as I am?
If I were a shepherd,
I would bring him a lamb.
If I were a wise man,
I would do my part –
Yet what I can I give him:
Give him my heart.

Christina Rossetti

Our Father in heaven,
Hallowed be your name.
Your kingdom come,
Your will be done,
On earth as it is in heaven.
Give us today our daily bread,
And forgive us our sins,
As we forgive those who sin against us.
Lead us away from temptation
And deliver us from evil,
For yours is the kingdom,
And the power, and the glory,
Forever and ever.
Amen

The prayer that Jesus taught his friends

Dear God,
Help me to be good
When I have to share my toys.
Help me to be good
When I'm making too much noise.
Help me to be good
And eat up all my greens.
Help me to be good
When I'm tempted to be mean.
Help me to be good
Each and every day.
Help me to be good
In every single way.

Original

Lord, may your spirit
Be nearer than breathing,
Nearer than any part,
Nearer to me than my own two feet;
May you live within my heart.

Original

Lord, make my heart a place
where angels sing!

John Keble

Oh make my heart so still, so still,
When I am deep in prayer,
That I might hear the white mist-wreaths
Losing themselves in air!

Utsonomya San, Japan

Teach me to do the thing that's right,
And when I sin, forgive,
And make it still my chief delight
To serve thee while I live.

Jane Taylor

Help me notice when people need a hand.
Help me see when they are sad and need a friend.

Original

Dear God, when I feel like a nobody,
help me remember that I am somebody to you.

Original

O God, make us children of quietness and heirs of peace.

St Clement

Jesus, may I
Walk your way
(point to feet)

In all I do
(hold out hands)

And all I say.
(touch finger to lips)

Original

Dear God,
I'm going to really try to be good as gold all day,
And nice to all my special friends when I go out to play.
If they say nasty things to me I mustn't do the same.
I don't want Mum to get annoyed – or give me the blame!
But, God, it isn't easy to be as nice as pie,
So I know that you will help me to really, really try!

Original

Father, help me see the world as you see it,
Help me live in the world as you would live,
Help me care about the world in all its troubles,
Help me play my part in making it better.

Original

This is me looking up at you.
Help me always be close to you.

Original

Day by day, dear Lord, of thee
Three things I pray:
To see thee more clearly,
To love thee more dearly,
To follow thee more nearly,
Day by day.

St Richard of Chichester

Help me to know what's wrong and what's right;
Help me to do good with all my might.

Original

Special Days

Dear God, this is Monday.
Help me start a good week.

Dear God, it's Tuesday.
It's still early in the week.
Be with me as I try to make it a good one.

Dear God, Wednesday already!
Halfway through the week.
Please bless all those I meet today.

Dear God, thank you for Thursday.
I've made a good start. Please help me
with the rest of the week.

Dear God, it's Friday.
Nearly the weekend! Time to look back on my week.
Thank you for being with me.

Dear God, it's Saturday – yippee!
So much to do, so little time.
Please bless all my friends today.

Dear God, it's Sunday, your day.
Happy day. Holy day. Thank you for the past week.
Please help me enjoy next week with you.

Original

Sunday should be a fun day,
Not a glum day.
Sunday should be a rest day,
Not a work day.

Original

All that we see rejoices in the sunshine,
All that we hear makes merry in the spring:
God grant us such a mind
To be glad after our kind,
And to sing his praises evermore for everything.

Christina Rossetti

Start each day with a fresh beginning;
as if this whole world was made anew.

From an Amish school

I go forth today
in the might of heaven,
in the brightness of the sun,
in the whiteness of snow,
in the splendour of fire,
in the speed of lightning,
in the swiftness of wind,
in the firmness of rock.
I go forth today
in the hand of God.

Irish prayer

It is the first day of school today.
Quite exciting, but a little bit scary.
Lord be with me in this term ahead.

Original

Tomorrow is a special day
I'm off on holiday – hooray!
I'm going where there's sand and sea,
And lots of treats for you and me.
Where ponies give rides on the beach,
And seagulls fly just out of reach.

Original

We've been packing our stuff,
We've been counting the days,
We've been saying goodbye
In a whole lot of ways.
It's a very special day – we're moving!
Please travel with us
As we leave our old home,
Please help us to know
That we're never alone.

Original

These candles on my cake,
I blow them out,
A wish I make.
To this wish
I add a prayer:
Please God, be with me
Everywhere.

Original

Love came down at Christmas,
Love all lovely, love divine;
Love was born at Christmas,
Star and angels gave the sign.

Christina Rossetti

Happy Birthday, Jesus!
Thank you for sharing your special day with us.
The kings brought you gifts, so we give presents.
Your family was happy, so we have parties and food.
Thank you for giving us Christmas.
Happy Birthday, Jesus!

Original

Jesus, who died for me,
Help me to live for thee.

Original

Dear Jesus, everyone thought you were dead. They took you down from the cross, with tears in their eyes and buried you in a cave with a big stone outside. Then they went home – the saddest people on Earth. Later, they went back with flowers, but they got such a shock. The stone was rolled away, the cave was empty, and you were walking in the garden. Then they were the happiest people on Earth. No wonder we are happy at Easter. We know that you're alive and always will be.

Original

Saying Sorry

The Bible says, don't let the sun go down on your anger. Dear Lord, when I have a fight with my friend, help us make up before we leave each other, because it will be much harder to say sorry the next day.

Original

O God,
I feel so bad,
I said some things
I shouldn't have.
I want to start
Again and say
With all my heart
I'm sorry.

Original

Something's gone wrong with this morning,
My pillow seems stuck to my head!
I'm in a bad mood,
I've gone right off my food,
And I don't want to get out of bed.
Dear God, can you help with this morning?
I really don't want to be sad.
Though the morning is grey,
This is a new day,
So perhaps things aren't really so bad!

Original

Sometimes I'm good,
But I can be bad.
Sometimes I'm happy,
Sometimes I'm sad.
Forgive me when I'm bad.

Original

I can be helpful,
I can be mean.
Sometimes I'm somewhere in between.
Help me do what I know I should do.
Help me choose to be good like you.
Forgive me when I'm mean.

Original

Dear God, today started badly and got worse, like a drawing that went wrong. Help me bring the drawing to you so that you can rub it out and give me a clean sheet of paper for tomorrow.

Original

Lord, I know I've been unkind.
I've hurt you and hurt my friend.
Help me to play nicely,
Sharing things and being caring,
Playing games, not calling names
But being good and kind.
And at day's end
Help me to pray nicely.

Original

I quarrelled with my friend today. I am sorry.
Help me to make it up to him/her.
Help me to be a better friend tomorrow.

Original

Keep me from being too busy to see
When someone needs help from someone like me.

Original

Dear God, I love secrets. Help me know when
I should keep a secret and when I should tell a secret.
And help me understand the difference between the two.

Original

Dear Father, thank you for today.
There were good parts I'd like to remember and bad parts I'd rather forget. Forgive me for the things I did wrong and help me to be better tomorrow. Thank you for all the good things and thank you for being with me in it all.

Original

O Lord, forgive the bad things I have done,
and show me how to be more like you.

Original

Goodnight Blessings

Jesus, saviour, wash away
All that has been wrong today:
Help me every day to be
Good and gentle, more like thee.

Frances Ridley Havergal

In peace I will both lie down and sleep, for you alone,
O Lord, make me to dwell in safety.

From Psalm 4

Alone with none but thee, my God,
I journey on my way.
What need I fear, when thou art near
O king of night and day?
More safe am I within thy hand
Than if a host did round me stand.

St Columba

Day is done,
Gone the sun
From the lake,
From the hills,
From the sky.
Safely rest,
All is well!
God is nigh.

Traditional

Glory be to thee, my God, this night,
For all the blessings of the light;
Keep me, O keep me, king of kings,
Beneath thine own almighty wings.

Original

Good night! Good night!
Far flies the light;
But still God's love
Shall flame above,
Making all bright.
Good night! Good night!

Victor Hugo

Matthew, Mark, Luke, and John,
Bless the bed that I lie on.
Four corners to my bed,
Four angels round my head,
One to watch and one to pray
And two to bear my soul away.

Traditional

Keep watch, dear Lord, with those who work,
or watch, or weep this night, and give your
angels charge over those who sleep.

St Augustine

Lord, when we have not any light,
And mothers are asleep,
Then through the stillness of the night
Thy little children keep.
When shadows haunt the quiet room,
Help us to understand
That thou art with us through the gloom,
To hold us by the hand.

Anne Matheson

Now I lay me down to sleep,
I pray the Lord my soul to keep.
If I should die before I wake,
I pray the Lord my soul to take.

Traditional

Lord, keep us safe this night,
Secure from all our fears;
May angels guard us while we sleep,
Till morning light appears.

John Leland

Jesus, tender shepherd, hear me,
Bless your little lamb tonight;
Through the darkness please be near me;
Keep me safe till morning light.

Mary Lundie Duncan

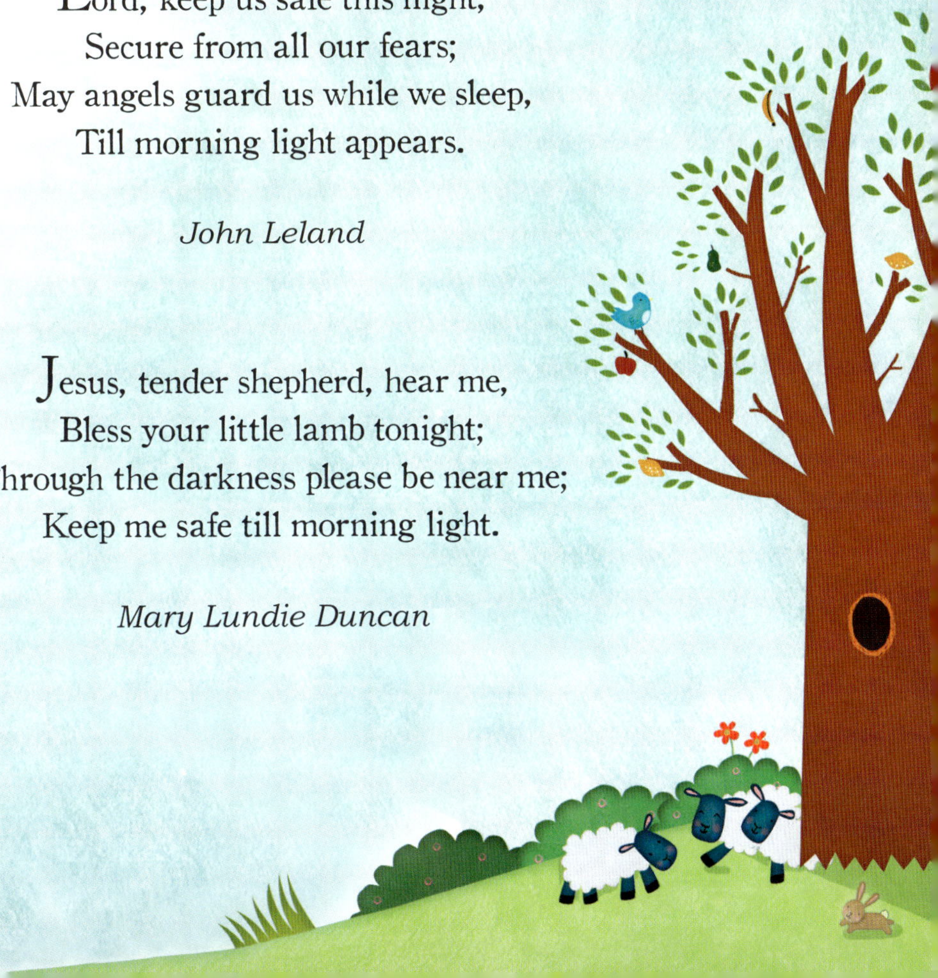

Peace of the running waves to you,
Deep peace of the flowing air to you,
Deep peace of the quiet Earth to you,
Deep peace of the shining stars to you,
Deep peace of the shades of night to you,
Moon and stars always giving light to you.
Deep peace of Christ, the Son of Peace, to you.

Traditional Gaelic blessing

God bless everyone in the whole wide world tonight. Guard us and guide us and help us love one another, so that your world can be a happy and peaceful place for all people.

Original

Give me peace in my heart, keep me praying,
Give me peace in my heart, I pray,
Give me peace in my heart, keep me praying,
Keep me praying till the end of day.

Traditional

The grace of the Lord Jesus Christ,
and the love of God, and the fellowship
of the Holy Spirit, be with
us all evermore.

Traditional blessing

Bible Stories by Theme

Festivals

Christmas

Palm Sunday

Passover

Easter

Jesus' Appearances and Ascension

Pentecost

Celebrations

Weddings

Babies

Jesus

The Life of Jesus

Themes

Going Wrong

Troubled Times

Messengers and Prophets

Journeys

Meetings

David's Music

The Temple

Returning to Jerusalem

The Early Church

Letters

Index of Bible Stories

Prayers: Index of First Lines